CATALOGUE

OF THE

Delta Upsilon Fraternity.

ΟΥΔΕΝ ΑΔΗΛΟΝ.

Utica, N. Y.
CURTISS & CHILDS, BOOK AND JOB PRINTERS,
Nos. 9 & 11 Fayette Street.
M DCCC LXVII.

CONSTITUTION

OF THE

Delta Upsilon Fraternity.

PREAMBLE.

Believing that Secret Societies are calculated to destroy the harmony of College, to create distinctions not founded on merit, to produce strife and animosity, we feel called upon to exert ourselves to counteract the evil tendency of such associations.

We believe that the evils resulting from them are such as can be suppressed only by action combined with principles.

We are confident that the great objects of equality, fraternity and morality may be attained without resorting to the veil of secrecy.

We, therefore, the several Anti-Secret Societies of Hamilton and Waterville Colleges, the University of Rochester, and Middlebury, Rutgers and Jefferson Colleges, in order to secure greater unity, permancy and efficiency of effort, do agree to form ourselves into a Fraternity, for the purpose of counteracting the evil tendency of secret associations in College, for maintaining and diffusing liberal principles, and for promoting intellectual, social and moral improvement.

In doing this, we trust that we have at heart the best interests of the Institutions to which we belong, and that we are directed by the light of experience, the suggestions of reason and the dictates of conscience.

We adopt, as our guide, the following

CONSTITUTION.

ARTICLE I.

NAME.

SEC. 1. This association shall be called the DELTA UPSILON FRATERITY.

SEC. 2. The several Societies constituting this Fraternity shall be denominated Chapters, and shall take their names from their respective Institutions.

ARTICLE II.

MEMBERSHIP.

SEC. 1. This Fraternity shall consist of active, graduate and honorary members.

SEC. 2. Any person may be admitted a member of this Fraternity, at a regular meeting of any Chapter, by the concurrence of not less than three-fourths of its active members.

SEC. 3. No person shall be admitted a member of this Fraternity, who does not practice strict morality, or who belongs to, or countenances any College secret society.

SEC. 4. Each candidate for active membership shall at his initiation into the Fraternity assent to the following

PLEDGE.

You affirm that the principles of this Fraternity, as expressed in its Preamble and Constitution, accord entirely with your views; that, as a member of this Fraternity, you will faithfully adhere to those principles and abide by all its rules and regulations; that you will ever extend to each brother the right hand of sympathy; that you will uphold and encourage your fellow members in all that is honorable and right; and that, at all times, and in all circumstances, you will endeavor to cultivate those feelings, which should ever exist between *brothers* engaged in a common cause;—all this you solemnly promise on your sacred honor.

SEC. 5. Any member, who violates the Pledge laid down in the fourth section of this article, shall be expelled from the Fraternity.

SEC. 6. No member shall be suspended or expelled from the Fraternity except by resolutions, concurred in by three-fourths of the members of his Chapter, present at the next regular meeting after their introduction.

SEC. 7. No resolution to suspend or expel a member shall be adopted, without affording him the privilege of defending himself; and the Secretary of the Chapter shall give him notice of the resolutions, as soon as possible after their introduction.

SEC. 8. During the consideration of resolutions to suspend or expel a member, he shall be considered, as under censure of the Fraternity, and, while under censure, shall not be allowed to enjoy the privileges or to perform the duties of a member.

SEC. 9. A copy of the resolutions suspending or expelling a member, signed by the President and Recording Secretary of the Chapter, shall be forwarded to the several Chapters.

SEC. 10. Any member in good standing may at any regular meeting of his Chapter receive an honorable dismission from the Fraternity by a unanimous vote of the members present.

ARTICLE III.

OFFICERS OF CHAPTERS.

SEC. 1. The officers of each Chapter shall consist of a President, Vice President, Corresponding Secretary, Recording Secretary, Treasurer and such other officers as the Chapter may deem necessary.

SEC. 2. The officers of each Chapter shall be chosen by a majority vote of its active members, at such time and for such term of office, as may be arranged by the Chapter: provided, however, that the term of office of the Corresponding Secretary shall not be less than one year.

SEC. 3. The President shall preside at all meetings of the Chapter; shall have power in any emergency to call a meeting; and during his absence, or other disability, the next highest officer present shall perform his duties *pro tempore.*

SEC. 4. The Vice President shall be President in case that office becomes vacant by the absence or other disability of the President.

SEC. 5. The Corresponding Secretary shall carry on all the correspondence of the Chapter with other Chapters of the Fraternity.

SEC. 6. The Recording Secretary shall keep a correct record of the proceedings of his Chapter.

SEC. 7. The Treasurer shall take charge of the finances of the Chapter.

ARTICLE IV.

OFFICERS OF THE FRATERNITY.

SEC. 1. The officers of the DELTA UPSILON FRATERNITY shall be a President, Vice President, and Secretary, who shall be elected at each regular convention of the Fraternity by a majority vote of the delegates present; their term of office expiring with the adjournment of the next regular convention after their election.

SEC. 2. The President of the Fraternity shall preside at all conventions; shall give notice to each Chapter of every convention of the Fraternity, at least three weeks previous to its meeting; shall make known to the several Chapters all amendments to this Constitution, and shall perform such other duties, as may devolve upon his office.

SEC. 3. The Vice President of the Fraternity shall perform the duties of President *pro tempore* in his absence or other disabillity.

SEC. 4. The Secretary of the Fraternity shall take charge of its finances; shall keep a correct record of each convention of the Fraternity in a book, provided for this purpose; shall forward a copy of the record of each convention to the several Chapters; and shall perform such other duties, as may devolve upon his office.

SEC. 5. The several Chapters to which these officers belong shall have power to fill vacancies when such occur.

ARTICLE V.

CONVENTIONS OF THE FRATERNITY.

SEC. 1. A Convention of the DELTA UPSILON FRATERNITY, consisting of delegates from the several Chapters, shall meet regularly once in each year at such time and place, as shall have been determined at the preceding regular convention of the Fraternity.

SEC. 2. A special convention may be called by the President of the Fraternity, at the request of any Chapter, to meet at such time and place as he may designate.

SEC. 3. Delegates to the conventions of the Fraternity shall be provided with certificates of their election, signed by the President and Recording Secretary of their respective Chapters, which shall be presented to the President of the Fraternity, at the meeting of the convention.

SEC. 4. Every delegate to the conventions of the Fraternity shall be entitled to one vote in all its deliberations, excepting when a vote by Chapters is called for by any delegate, in which case, no Chapter shall have more than one vote.

SEC. 5. Delegates from a majority of the Chapters to any convention shall constitute a quorum, without which no business, transacted by the convention, shall be valid unless ratified by a majority of the Chapters.

SEC. 6. The Fraternity, at any convention, may make such rules as it may consider necessary for the government of its conventions, provided they do not conflict with the provisions of this Constitution.

ARTICLE VI.

RELATIONS OF CHAPTERS.

SEC. 1. All applications from societies desiring to be admitted into the Fraternity, shall be forwarded to the President of the Fraternity to be submitted by him to the next convention, or to the three senior Chapters, as he may deem expedient.

SEC. 2. New Chapters may be admitted into the Fraternity by the unanimous vote of any convention, or by the concurrence of the three senior Chapters, subject to the ratification of the Fraternity at its next convention.

SEC. 3. The President of the Fraternity shall appoint a committee, who shall proceed to the society to be admitted and administer the Pledge, laid down in the fourth Section of the second Article of this Constitution, to the members of the new Chapter, and establish it in conformity with all the provisions of this Constitution ; reporting in writing to each Chapter of the Fraternity.

SEC. 4. Each Chapter shall inform the several Chapters of the Fraternity of the decease or honorable dismission of any of its members.

SEC. 5. A Triennial Catalogue of the Fraternity, containing this Constitution and the names of all members of the Fraternity, arranged under their respective Chapters shall be published by the senior Chapter.

SEC. 6. The Badge and Insignia of the Fraternity shall be uniform throughout the several Chapters.

SEC. 7. The several Chapters shall communicate with each other by letter, at least once a term.

SEC. 8. Every active member of the Fraternity shall be bound by his honor as a gentleman to attend all meetings of his Chapter.

SEC. 9. At all meetings of the several Chapters a majority of the active members shall constitute a quorum, without which no business shall be transacted.

ARTICLE VII.

ADDITIONAL REGULATIONS.

SEC. 1. Each Chapter may adopt such By-Laws for its own government as it may consider expedient, provided they do not conflict with the provisions of this Constitution, or the acts of the Fraternity in its conventions.

SEC. 2. All acts of the Fraternity in its conventions shall have equal power and force with this Constitution, provided they do not conflict with its provisions.

ARTICLE VIII.

AMENDMENTS.

This Constitution may be amended by resolutions adopted by two-thirds of all the Chapters of the Fraternity; such resolutions having been adopted in convention, or forwarded in writing to the President of the Fraternity.

Chapters.

WILLIAMS,	Williams College, Mass.
UNION,	Union College, N. Y.
AMHERST,	Amherst College, Mass.
HAMILTON,	Hamilton College, N. Y.
WATERVILLE,	Waterville College, Me.
ROCHESTER,	Rochester University, N. Y.
MIDDLEBURY,	Middlebury College, Vt.
BOWDOIN,	Bowdoin College, Me.
RUTGERS,	New Brunswick, N. J.
JEFFERSON,	Canonsburg, Pa.
NEW YORK,	New York City.
WESTERN RESERVE	Hudson, O.
MADISON,	Hamilton, N. Y.
WASHINGTON,	Washington, Pa.

Williams Chapter.

Founded in 1834.

MEMBERS.

Names.	*Class.*	*Residences.*
	1836.	
*Algernon S. Baldwin,		Great Barrington, Mass.
Rev. Hiram Bell,		Killingworth, Conn.
Rev. Philo Canfield,		Bridgeport, Conn.
Rev. Elias Clark,		Greenville, N. Y.
Rev. T. Jarvis Clark,		East Cummington, Mass.
*George Clisby,		Medford, Mass.
Rev. Samuel D. Darling,		Cummington, Mass.
Anson L. Hobart,		Worcester, Mass.
Rev. E. William Kellogg,		Millville, N. Y.
Rev. Joshia Lyman,		Lenox, Mass.
Henry Morgan,		Macon, Ga.
Lyndon G. Lyman,		Newark, N. J.
Rev. Lebeus R. Phillips,		Sharon, Mass.
Zalmon Richards,		Washington, D. C.
John H. Westfall,		Wantage, N. J.
Rev. Edmund Wright,		St. Louis, Mo.
Charles G. Wright,		New Orleans, La.
		XVII.
	1837.	
Edward F. Brooks,		Gill, Mass.
*Rev. Daniel Brown,		Carmel, N. Y.
Rev. Edward Clark,		Chesterfield, Mass.
Rev. Solomon Clark,		Plainfield, Mass.
Edward S. Clarke, M. D.		New York City.

* Deceased.

S. Johnson Field,	New York City.
John P. Hills,	Ohio.
Rev. Lewis C. Lockwood,	New Windsor, N. Y.
William H. Noble,	Cleveland, Ohio.
Rev. Eber M. Rollo,	Stephentown, Mass.
*Comfort Sparks,	Sheffield, Mass.
T. Wilder Tappan,	Brooklyn, N. Y.
George M. Turner,	Detroit, Mich.

XIII.

1838.

Davis Alton,	Pittston, Penn.
Rev. Willard Brigham,	Ashfield, Mass.
William Bross, Lt Gov. Ill.	Chicago, Ill.
Cole Herman Denio,	West Troy, N. Y.
William N. Edwards,	Dayton, Ohio.
Rev. Thomas A. Hall,	Otis, Mass.
Frederick H. Hastings,	Albany, N. Y.
*Edward P. Hawks,	Milton, N. C.
Rowland Sears Howes,	Troy, N. Y.
*Rev. Foster Lilley,	Andover, Mass.
Theophilus Page,	Rahway, N. J.
Rev. Charles Peabody,	Biddeford, Me.
Rev. David Pease,	Manlius, N. Y.
Rev. Francis Williams,	Chaplin, Ct.

XIV.

1839.

John M. Brewster, Jr.,	Longmeadow, Mass.
Edward A. Dickinson,	Jamestown, N. Y.
Wiley R. Ellis,	Sandwich, Mass.
Jonathan Ford,	Madison, Wis.
Charles G. Hazeltine,	Cherry Valley, N. Y.
Edmund B. Jennings,	New London, Ct.
Rev. Jonathan S. Judd,	Middlebury, Ct.
Rev. GEORGE KERR,	Franklin, N. Y.
Rev. Nathaniel Lassels,	Exeter, N. H.
Rev. William M. Legate,	Oak Grove, Ct.
Rev. Addison Lyman,	Genesco, Ill.
William Ward Mitchell,	Cummington, Mass.
John Nichols,	Janesville, Wis.
Franklin Potter, M. D.	Charlemont, Mass.
David J. Pratt,	New York City.
Zenas M. Phelps,	Sing Sing, N. Y.
Rev. Levi Rose,	Howard, N. Y.

R. C. Robinson,	Troy, N. Y.
Lucian Royes,	New Marlborough, Mass.
Rev. Townsend Walker,	Huntington, Mass.
Rev. William J. White,	Michigan City, Ill.
Rev. Samuel J. White,	Canonsville, N. Y.
Hon. E. MONROE WRIGHT, Secretary of State.	Williamsburg, Mass.,

XXIII.

1840.

James Watson Brown,	Belleville, N. Y.
James M. Burt,	Cortlandville, N. Y.
George M. Cady,	Oswego, N. Y.
Barnabas Collins,	Newark, N. J.
Augustus Cornwall,	Brooklyn, N. Y.
*Rev. Oliver Dimon,	Andover Theo. Seminary.
Hon. Charles N. Emerson,	Great Barrington, Mass.
Hiram W. Farnsworth,	New London, Ct.
*J. C. Fowler,	South Carolina.
Rev. D. D. Frost,	Reading, Ct.
Thomas G. Gardner,	Galveston, Texas.
Rev. Charles Hawley,	Genoa, N. Y.
Rev. Samuel Newell Hill,	Troy, Mich.
Edward M. Jordan,	Knoxville, Ill.
George McClelland,	Rensselaerville, N. Y.
Charles Whittlesey,	New York City.
Rev. Eliphalet Whittlesey,	Salisbury, Ct.

XVII.

1841.

Edwin C. Bidwell, M. D.,	Keene, Ohio.
Rev. H. B. Blake,	Belchertown, Mass.
Rev. Luther Clapp,	Wauwatosa, Wis.
Rev. O. Wellington Cooley,	Fond Du Lac, Wis.
Alvin Devereaux,	Deposit, N. Y.
William Hills,	Auburn, N. Y.
S. W. Fisher,	Westhampton, Mass.
Rev. James Herrick,	Madura, Hindostan.
Rev. William A. Keith,	Missouri.
J. Edwards Lee, M. D.	Philadelphia, Pa.
James Little, Jr.,	South Middletown, N. Y.
*Henry L. Marsh,	Racine, Wis.
Rev. Enos Montague,	Summit, Wis.
*Rev. Eugene W. Pugsley,	Ghent, N. Y.
Rev. Nathaniel E. Pierson,	Weston, N. Y.

*Samuel D. Rogers,	New York City.
W. H. Rolloson,	Williamsburg, Va.
A. Worthington Taylor,	Warren, Conn.
James Sedgwick,	Great Barrington, Mass.
*Ephraim Tenney,	Dummerston, Vt.
Joseph Warner,	Northampton, Mass.
John G. Warren,	Troy, N. Y.
Moses Warren, Jr.,	Troy, N. Y.
Russell M. Wright,	Washington, Ga.

XXIV.

1842.

Rev. ADDISON BALLARD,	Williamstown, Mass.
Rev. Thomas Scott Bacon,	New Orleans, La.
Elisha B. Bassett,	Allegan, Mich.
Rev. William A. Benton,	Syrian Mission.
James Brewer,	Brandon, Miss.
John Griswold Buel,	Troy, N. Y.
William H. Edwards,	New York City.
Rev. G. R. Entler,	Erie, Pa.
*Rev. Henry A. Ford, M. D.,	Gaboon, Africa.
S. Hildreth Foster,	Rensselaerville, N. Y.
Rev. William Goodwin,	Huntington, Ct.
William A. Hawley, M. D.	Waterown, N. Y.
E. Andrews Hubbard,	Easthampton, Mass.
Charles Edmond Jenkins,	Albany, N. Y.
Jonathan LeFevere,	New Paltz, N. Y.
*Rev. E. G. Johnson,	New York City.
Rev. Horace Lyman,	Portland, Oregon.
John H. Kellom,	East Bloomfield, N. Y.
*Charles H. Lyon,	Auburn, N. Y.
Rev. Dwight W. Marsh,	Mosul, Asia.
Rev. Henry Osborn,	Hunter, N. Y.
Rev. H. M. Scudder,	Arcot, India.
Andrew G. Riley,	Lyman, N. Y.
*Rev. John H. Sage,	Fredonia, N. Y.
*Rev. O. Maynard Sears,	Dalton, Mass.
James S. Slighter,	New York City.
Rev. J. Torrey Smith,	Amherst, Mass.
*Franklin C. Strong,	Northampton, Mass.
Lyman F. Wilcox,	Monticello, Ga.

XXIX.

1843.

GEORGE F. BIGELOW, M. D., Boston, Mass.
REUBEN B. BOIES, Portland, Oregon.
R. COLTON BRAINARD, New York City.
*Rev. GEORGE CLARK, New York City.
*CHARLES K. CLARK, Baltimore, Md.
*HIRAM CHASE, Chester, N. H.
Rev. THEODORE COOKE, Northampton, Mass.
Rev. ALEXANDER DILLEY, Rodman, N. Y.
Rev. J. BOGARDUS DONELLY, New York City.
W. EARL FLING, Charleston, N. H.
C. H. FOUNTAIN, M. D., California.
DANIEL C. GREEN, New York City.
Rev. H. B. HOSFORD, Hudson, Ohio.
Prof. Rhet. and Intel. Phil., Western Reserve College.
J. OTIS M. INGERSOLS, M. D., Ithaca, N. Y.
EDMUND B. JENNINGS, New London, Ct.
Rev. LEWIS JESSUP, Northfield, Ct.
*HENRY KELLOGG, Rockingham, Vt.
Rev. EDWARD LORD, Adams, N. Y.
E. BELCHER MEAD, Greenwich, Ct.
*IRA P. OSBORN, Windham, N. Y.
J. S. POLER, Medina, N. Y.
TARRANT SIBLEY, Bennington, Vt.
L. W. SAVAGE, Springfield, Ohio.
Rev. LUCIUS E. SMITH, Lewisburg, Pa.
*Rev. J. C. STRONG, Chester Factories.
E. C. TOMPKINS, New York City.
Hon. OLIVER WARNER, Northampton, Mass.
Secretary of State.
*ALDEN BARR VINING, Plainfield, Mass.
SAMUEL E. WARNER, New York City.
Rev. JOSEPH K. WRIGHT, Troy, N. Y.
XXX.

1844.

HENRY J. BARKER, South Adams, Mass.
CYRUS BENTLEY, Chicago, Ill.
Rev. JACOB BEST, Waymart, Pa.
HENRY P. COON, M. D., San Francisco, Cal.
AMBROSE N. DANFORTH, M. D., Maine.
WILLIAM J. DAVIS, Coleraine, Mass.
ISAAC DE LA MATER, Lockland, Ohio.
CHARLES DEMOND, Boston, Mass.

Rev. J. Edwards Ford,	Syrian Mission.
James Green,	Monson, Mass.
Cyrus Guffin,	Carlisle, N. Y.
Calvin C. Halsey, M. D.,	Nicholson, Pa.
Joseph B. Hawkes,	St. Josephs, La.
Rev. THERON H. HAWKS,	Cleveland, O.
Julius W. Hubbard,	Baltimore, Md.
Alexander M. Huling,	Bennington, Vt.
Thomas Scott Lambert, M. D.	New York City.
Josiah Lassell, M. D.	Auburndale, Mass.
John P. Lansing,	Cohoes, N. Y.
*Samuel M. Lassell,	West Stockbridge, Mass.
John E. Mann,	Schoharie, N. Y.
*Calvin W. Marsh,	Racine, Wis.
L. M. Meeker,	Rahway, N. J.
Rev. Cryus T. Mills,	San Francisco, Cal.
Edward N. S. Morgan, M. D.,	Pownal, Vt.
*Martin S. Pixley,	Plainfield, Mass.
Rev. David Rood,	Zulu Mission, South Africa.
*William L. Silcox,	Culpepper Court House, Va.
J. Sanford Smith,	Elizabethtown, N. J.
James H. Spellman,	Brooklyn, N. Y.
Edward R. Tinker,	North Adams, Mass.
Henry A. Tuttle,	Morristown, N. J.
James M. Wilson, M. D.,	Washington, D. C.
John C. Wolcott,	Cheshire, Mass.
Rev. Aaron R. Wolfe,	Montclair, N. Y.
	xxxv.

1845.

Nelson F. Atkins,	Westfield, Mass.
Rev. Henry Martin Bacon,	Philadelphia, Pa.
Rev. Henry W. Baldwin,	West Granville, Mass.
*Charles Brewster,	Williamstown, Mass.
Rev. Charles D. Buck,	Peekskill, N. Y.
Rev. Stephen Bush,	Waterford, N. Y.
Rev. Anson Clark,	Wisconsin.
George R. Cowles,	Norwalk, Ct.
Theodore J. Denton,	New York City.
Rev. William W. Eddy,	Syrian Mission.
Rev. Abraham Gosman,	Lawrenceville, N. J.
C. M. Hall,	New York City.
George Hodges,	Savannah, Ga.

Willard Hodges,	Rochester, N. Y.
Joel A. Jennings,	California.
*Benjamin McClure,	Bloomsburg, Pa.
Rev. Samuel L. Merrill,	Theresa, N. Y.
A. D. Nichols,	Ithaca, N. Y.
Rev. Benjamin F. Relya,	Fall River, Mass.
William B. Rice,	Norfolk, Ct.
G. Lafayette Squire,	Holyoke, Mass.
George Stone,	Elizabethtown, N. J.
*Ambrose T. Tilson,	Cummington, Mass.
Titus T. Wadsworth,	Henniker, Me.
*Lewis White,	Williamstown, Mass.
Rev. H. A. Wilder,	Zulu Mission, S. Africa.
William P. White,	Longmeadow, Mass.
	XXVII.

1846.

*Erastus Anderson,	Ware, Mass.
*Rev. Charles B. Ball,	Wilton, Conn.
*Rev. Frederick A. Brewster,	Canton, China.
Eri Bogardus,	Texas.
John C. Clegg,	New York City.
Rev. George W. Coan,	Nestorian Mission.
Gabriel Grant, M. D.,	Newark, N. J.
George A. Haynes,	New York City.
Charles L. Hubbell, M. D.,	Troy, N. Y.
Rev. Allyn Stanley Kellogg,	Vernon, Ct.
*Leander Kipp,	Troy, N. Y.
Thomas A. Lovell,	Phillipston, Mass.
Emmons T. Mockridge,	Philadelphia, Pa.
Isaiah H. Nutting, M. D.	Oxford, N. H.
*Increase B. Page,	Pittsfield, Mass.
Joel S. Page,	Chicago, Ill.
Lawton S. Parsons,	Easthampton, L. I.
Edward S. Pugsley,	Ghent, N. Y.
Rev. Daniel S. Rodman,	Hartford, Ct.
Andrew M. Smith, M. D.,	Williamstown, Mass.
Rev. Marshall D. Sanders,	Ceylon Mission.
William M. Sayre, M. D.,	Marysville, Cal.
Rev. David A. Strong,	South Deerfield, Mass.
James M. Tuthill,	Greenport, L. I.
Rev. Elisha Whittlesey,	Waterbury, Ct.
	XXV.

1847.

Rev. Charles F. Bacon,	Union, N. Y.
*William D. Blanchard,	Groton, Mass.
Lewis W. Bryant,	Elizabethtown, N. J.
Rev. Uzal W. Condit,	Deerfield, N. H.
Rev. Thomas S. Dewing,	Blauveltville, N. Y.
Rev. George P. Folsom,	Geneseo, N. Y.
Rev. CHARLES H. GARDNER,	New York City,
Principal of the Ferris Institute.	
J. Manning Hosford, M. D.,	Racine, Wis.
Andrew Lansing,	Cohoes, N. Y.
Rev. I. NEWTON LINCOLN,	Williamstown, Mass.,
Professor of Latin and French, Williams College.	
Rev. Elihu Loomis,	Littleton, Mass.
Rev. Judson G. Lyman,	New Hartford, Ct.
*Rev. Charles H. Norton,	N. Becket, Mass.
JOHN L. T. PHILLIPS,	Williamstown, Mass.
Lawrence Prof. of Greek Language and Literature, Williams College.	
Lyman D. Prindle,	Nebraska City.
Rev. Thomas H. Rouse,	Jamestown, N. Y.
Rev. Charles B. Sheldon,	Excelsior, Wis.
Thomas Ward Stafford,	Australia.
H. Boardman Smith,	Elmira, N. Y.
Nathaniel E. Taylor,	Rupert, Vt.
A. B. W. Van Vechten,	New York City.
*John B. Waterman,	Williamstown, Mass.
David A. Wells,	Boston, Mass.

XXIII.

1848.

Warren C. Benton,	Nassau, N. Y.
Henry Bradford,	Tallahassee, Fa.
Albert H. Bodman,	Greenfield, Mass.
William H. Bradford, M. D.,	Tallahassee, Fa.
Rev. Thomas S. Bradley,	Cornwall, Ct.
Rev. Edgar W. Clark,	Milton, N. Y.
Rev. George W. Connit,	Deep River, Ct.
Rev. Eli Corwin,	Honolulu, S. I.
Edwin Davenport,	Boston, Mass.
Jacob B. Dewell,	Pine Plains, N. Y.
Rev. CHARLES S. DUNNING,	Honesdale Pa.
Derick De Freest,	Bristol, R. I.
*Noah D. Gardner,	Hancock, Mass.
Rev. T. C. P. Hyde,	Bolton, Ct.

Samuel T. Field,	Shelburne Falls, Mass.
Chandler T. Ford,	Iowa City.
T. Cadwell Ingalls,	Orange, N. Y.
Thomas J. King,	Easthampton, L. I.
Joseph Keeney, M. D.,	Sand Lake, N. Y.
Rev. Arunah H. Lilly,	East Palmyra, N. Y.
*Henry E. Lord,	Norwich, Ct.
John G. McMynn,	Southport, Wis.
Charles D. Mills, M. D.,	Pittsfield, Mass.
John Reed,	Milton, S. C.
William P. Porter,	North Adams, Mass.
Hon. AMBROSE RYDER,	Carmel, N. Y.
Rev. John D. Strong,	Iowa City, Iowa.
Julius S. Townsend,	Troy, N. Y.
*Henry Wells,	Stockbridge, Mass.

XXIX.

1849.

E. G. BECKWITH,	Honolulu, Sandwich Is.,
President of Oahu College.	
James A. Bell,	New York City.
John M. Bacheldor,	Newbury, Ohio.
Bisbee Morell Beales,	Fairview, Pa.
*Fisher Ames Boies,	Blanford, Mass.
Evelyn A. Burt,	Pittsfield, Mass.
Rev. Albert Chamberlain,	Amenia, N. Y.
Edwin H. Van Deusen, M. D.,	New York City.
George Monger Coan,	Medina, N. Y.
Cyrus M. Dodd,	Alleghany City.
Professor of Mathematics in Ind. University.	
Edward J. Ford,	Athens, Pa.
Rev. Joseph C. Foster,	Springfield, Mass.
Rev. T. A. Hazen,	Dalton, Mass.
Rev. C. W. Higgins,	Big Flats, N. Y.
*Rev. James B. Howard,	Pittsfield, Mass.
W. Franklin Hurlburt,	South Lee, Mass.
Nathan S. King, M. D.,	New York City.
Henry C. Morris,	Gordon, N. Y.
Rev. John S. Nelson,	Williamstown, Ala.
Rev. John Newbanks,	Troy, N. Y.
John M. Newton,	———, Ohio.
Isaac G. Ogden,	Sand Lake, N. Y.
David S. Pierce,	Pittsfield, Mass.
*Newton H. Rosseter,	Great Barrington, Mass.

William D. Putnam,	West Brattleboro, Vt.
Francis Rand,	Roxbury, Mass.
Lynden A. Smith,	Newark, N. J.
Rev. Joseph D. Strong,	California.
Milton B. Whitney,	Westfield, Mass.

XXIX.

1850.

Frederick A. Curtiss,	———, California.
*Zebina Curtiss,	Pittsfield, Mass.
Oliver B. Hayes,	Dalton, Mass.
William Kerr,	South Middletown, N. Y.
Robert B. Moorman,	Fancy Hill, Va.
Rev. William E. Merriman,	———, Illinois.
Rev. P. Mason Bartlett,	Williamstown, N. Y.
Alfred J. Olds,	Wisconsin.
Albert M. Pratt,	Ravenna, Ohio.
William D. Porter,	New York City.
*T. F. Van Vechten,	New York City.
A. K. SMITH, M. D., Surgeon U. S. A.	New Smyrna, Fa.,
J. H. Sprague.	Greenfield, Mass.
*Robert M. Smith,	Sheffield, Mass.
*Elias E. Warner,	Canaan, N. Y.

XV.

1851.

Jarvis M. Adams,	Cleveland, Ohio.
Rufus J. Bell,	New York City.
S. H. Curtis,	West Stockbridge, Mass.
Abner DeWitt,	South Hadley, Mass.
Rev. Prescott B. Fay,	Lancaster, N. H.
Ephraim Flint, Jr.,	Westfield, Mass.
Rev. J. Lorenzo Lyons,	Montrose, Pa.
Rev. William A. Nyles,	Corning, N. Y.
Luther H. Northrop,	Haverstraw, N. Y.
*John Seymour,	Danville, Ill.
James White,	Boston, Mass.

XI.

1852.

O. D. Allis,	Chelsea, Vt.
Thomas A. Bradford, Jr.,	Tallahassee, Fa.
Simeon Batchellor,	Pownal, Vt.
Rowan Clark,	Huntington, Pa.
Charles H. Dann,	Franklin, N. Y.

F. F. Ford,	Newark Valley, N. Y.
Charles E. Harwood,	———, Illinois.
Norman L. Johnson,	Pittsfield, Mass.
John Adams Kilburn,	East Haddam, Ct.
George M. Noyes,	Buffalo, N. Y.
James M. Parsons,	New York City.
*William S. Potter,	Choctaw Mission.
Rev. S. C. Pixley,	Zulu Mission, S. Africa.
Henry L. Pratt,	———, Michigan.
Lewellyn Pratt,	Philadelphia, Pa.
T. P. Ranney,	Newark, N. J.
Rev. B. N. Seymour,	Centreville, California.
Alden B. Whipple,	Nantucket, Mass.
	XVIII.

1853.

Rev. Robert J. Adams,	Wallingford, Ct.
G. E. BECKWITH,	Honolulu, Sand. Islands.,
Professor of Languages, Oahu College.	
Andrew C. Blackmer,	St. Charles, Ill.
Rev. James A. Clark,	———, Michigan.
John D. English,	Red Hook, N. Y.
George Hazeltine,	Jamestown, N. Y.
Rev. H. A. Minor,	———, Maine.
Benjamin F. Munn,	Charleston, Ill.
Charles H. Reed,	Pittsfield, Mass.
James S. Woods,	Geneva, N. Y.
	X.

1854.

Richard K. Adams,	Hinsdale, Mass.
Rev. Judson Aspinwall,	Keokuk, Iowa.
Rev. Walter H. Clark,	Spencertown.
Rev. Samuel B. Forbes,	Manchester, Ct.
Rev. Horace B. Fosket,	Joilet, Ill.
Herman M. Glass,	Lyman, N. Y.
Rev. J. Hurd Strong,	East Windsor, Ct.
Rev. R. B. Snowdon,	New York City.
Horace H. Taft,	Pittsburg, Pa.
J. Judson Tucker,	New Bedford, Mass.
William Wells,	Wyalusing, Pa.
	XI.

1855.

John D. English,	Barrytown, N. Y.
J. P. S. Gifford,	Canaan, N. Y.

Alpha D. Griswold,	Southport, N. Y.
Marcus N. Horton,	Coventry, N. Y.
Henry C. Merritt,	Carmel, N. Y.
Alonzo Knapp,	Carmel, N. Y.
E. L. Lincoln,	North Adams, Mass.
Rev. Eldridge Mix,	New York City,
Martin H. Moore,	Dummerston, Vt.
James Orton,	Lisle, N. Y.
Rev. George W. Northrop, President of Chicago University.	Chicago, Ill.
S. Francis Shaw,	New Hartford, Ct.
Jarvis Rockwell,	Pittsfield, Mass.
Rev. Lyman Warner,	Ashfield, Mass.
Alvin Wallace,	Auburn, N. Y.
George T. Washburn,	Lenox, Mass.

XVI.

1856.

JAMES A. GARFIELD, Principal of the Western Reserve Eclectic Institute.	Hiram, Ohio.,
Abner Hazeltine, Jr.,	Jamestown, N. Y.
James K. Hazen,	Prattville, Ala.
Charles W. MacCarthy,	Potsdam, N. Y.
Phineas Mixter, Jr.,	Lane Theo. Seminary.
James McLean,	Glasgow, Scotland.
Edwin H. Pound,	Canandaigua, N. Y.
Frank Shepard,	North Adams, Mass.
L. P. Webber,	Salem, N. J.
Charles D. Wilbur,	Auburn, Ohio.
Lavalette Wilson,	New York City.

XI.

1857.

Rufus Apthorp,	Auburn Theo. Seminary.
Samuel E. Elmore,	Great Barrington, Mass.
James Guthrie,	York, N. Y.
Irvin MaGee,	Hudson, N. Y.
Robert E. McMath,	Rochester, N. Y.
Andrew Parsons,	Richfield.
Charles M. Pierce,	Hinsdale, Mass.
Charles A. Stork,	Andover Theo. Seminary.
Alexander Walker,	Caledonia, N. Y.
Horace H. Wells,	Hinsdale, Mass.

X.

1858.

Robert Emmet Adams,	Cleveland, Ohio.

Benjamin Bissel,	
Charles H. Bissel,	East Windsor Theo. Sem.
Joseph P. Bixby,	Union Theo. Seminary.
Charles H. Brown,	Troy, N. Y.
Truman T. Buck,	Cheshire, Mass.
Henry T. Ford,	Union Theo. Seminary.
Henry Herrick,	Twinsburg, Ohio.
William A. Lloyd,	
Charles C. C. Painter,	Draper's Valley, Va.
Edward A. Pierce,	Chicago, Ill.
Thomas Post,	Lenox, Mass.
Elias Fitch Tanner,	Hoosic Falls, N. Y.
	XIII.

1859.

Henry C. Haskell,	Huntington, Ohio.
Jeremiah D. Hyde,	Rondout, N. Y.
Henry A. Schauffler,	Constantinople, Turkey.
	III.

1860.

William A. Briggs,	Williamstown, Mass.
William W. Chapin,	Somers, Ct.
James H. Harwood,	Bennington, Vt.
Jasper Hutchings,	Brewer, Me.
George R. Leavitt,	Lowell, Mass.
Albert C. Reed,	Albany, N. Y.
	VI.

1861.

William P. Alcott,	Auburndale, Mass.
Edward N. Beale,	Spencertown, N. Y.
Thomas E. Brastow,	Brewer Village, Me.
George M. Carrington,	Winchester Centre, Conn.
Joseph Danielson,	West Killingly, Conn.
Chauncey Goodrich,	Hinsdale, Mass.
Benjamin F. Hastings,	Lenox, Mass.
Frederick Hicks,	Bennington, Vt.
George C. Reynolds,	East Windsor Hill, Conn.
George G. Smith,	Pittsburg, Pa.
Thomas J. Smith,	Salem, N. J.
William C. Spellman,	Brooklyn, N. Y.
George White,	Huntington, Canada East.
	XIII.

1862.

J. Albert Blake,	Swanton, Vt.
Edward R. Cutler,	Sudbury, Mass.

John Howard Goodhue,	Natick, Mass.
Reuben G. Hazen, Jr.,	Canterbury, Ct.
Wm. Albert James,	West Killingly, Ct.
Alexander M. Merwin,	New York City.
Albert Monroe Moore,	Lowell, Mass.
Frank E. Nettleton,	Fulton, N. Y.
Henry T. Perry,	Ashfield, Mass.
Frank H. Snow,	Fitchburg, Mass.
Leavitt W. Spring,	Manchester.

Union Chapter.

Founded in 1838.

MEMBERS.

Names.	*Class.*	*Residences.*
	1838.	
Hon. William Alexander,		Mobile, Ala.
John P. Allen,		Sturbridge, Mass.
James M. Austin, M. D.,		Waterford.
George Bartlett,		Binghamton.
William C. Benedict, M. D.,		Brooklyn, L. I.
Hiram Bennett,		Hornellsville.
John M. Bird, M. D.,		Chicago.
Austin Blair,		Jackson, Mich.
Rev. George Bugbee,		Sandusky, O.
Rev. Peter Burghardt,		West Farms.
Rev. James F. Calkins,		Wellsboro', Pa.
John W. Carey,		Racine, Wis.
Rev. J. F. Chamberlain,		New York City.
*Rev. Edward W. Champlin,		Saybrook, Ct.
Darwin Chichester,		Mount Morris.
Rev. William C. Child,		Farmingham, Mass.
Rev. George W. Clark,		New York City.
George W. Clark,		Bern.
Rev. Timothy Conklin,		New York City.
Rev. Augustus W. Cowles, President of Elmira Female College.		Elmira, N. Y.
Beebe D. Crary,		Elgin, Ill.
Rev. John R. Davis,		Blairstone, N. J.
Rev. Ephraim Deyoe,		Guilderland.

Rev. John Donaldson,	Greenville, Ky.
Rev. John Dubois,	Cicero, Corner.
Sherman Eddy, M. D.,	Lexington, Mo.
Rev. Thomas T. Farrington,	Salem.
James Fanning,	New York City.
Rev. James P. Fisher,	Johnstown.
Anthony C. Fonda,	Memphis, Tenn.
George C. Finch, M. D.,	Croton Falls.
Robert Fuller, M. D.,	Schenectady.
Rev. John Gardiner,	Harlingen, Vt.
A. B. Gardiner,	Pownal, Vt.
George A. Gates,	Rodman.
*Rev. Emery C. Green,	Kirkland, O.
Rev. David B. Hall,	Cleveland, O.
Rev. Horace Hendee,	Milledgeville, Ga.
Rev. Thomas M. Hodgman,	York, N. Y.
*Rev. Henry H. Hopkins,	Auburn.
Amos G. Hull,	Fulton.
*George W. Hustin,	Mayville.
Peltia Jakeway,	Fort Ann.
James H. Jansen,	Goshen.
*William Kelley, M. D.,	New York City.
Rev. William C. Kenyon,	Alfred Center.
Hon. George W. Kretsinger,	Sycamore.
Rev. William M. Legate,	Huntsville, Ala.
Cyrus Lyon,	Ohio.
Rev. David C. Lyon,	Bedford.
Rev. William F. Lockwood,	Fairfield C. H., Va.
Rev. Giles Manwaring, Jr.,	Somers.
Rev. Stephen Mattoon,	Bankok, Siam.
*Rev. William R. McChesney,	Lexington, Ky.
Hugh W. McClellan,	Chatham.
James Magoffin,	Lansingburg.
Rev. Peter A. McMartin,	Fredericksburg, Va.
Archibald McMartin,	Amsterdam.
*James P. Morange,	Albany.
Rev. Charles M. Morehouse,	Allegan, Mich.
Jarvis Mobray,	North Hempstead, L. I.
John W. Nelson,	New York City.
J. Oakly Nodyne,	New York.
P. G. Parker,	Buffalo.

Rev. B. P. Parry,	Ellsworth, Ct.
William Patten,	Lyons.
Rev. William K. Platt,	Sweden.
*Frederick W. Powell,	Trenton.
Henry K. Raymond,	Oshkosh, Wis.
Rev. Charles Richards,	Maumee City, O.
Rev. Ambrose S. Rogers,	Cornwall, Ct.
Rev. Joseph Rosencranks,	Onondaga Valley.
John Rosenbury,	Sharon.
Andrew Ross,	Pittsburg, Pa.
Jacob Sand,	Knox.
Isaac A. Saxton,	Pomfret, Vt.
Rev. Henry M. Selmer,	Louisville, Ky.
Rev. Lyman Sewall,	Sumner, Me.
James Small,	Cambridge.
W. K. Smith,	Versailles, Ky.
Rev. Cyrus Smith,	Wilmington, Vt.
John M. Stevenson,	Coila.
Robert Stickney,	Mount Hope.
Rev. John B. Stoddard,	Sherman, Ct.
Cornelius W. Stootkoff, M. D.	Newton, L. I.
John H. Storrs,	New York.
David Thayer, M. D.	Boston, Mass.
Rev. George H. Thatcher,	Ballston Center.
George Thompson,	Williamsburg.
John I. Tyler,	New York.
Eldert T. Tan Alstine,	Belvidere, Ill.
John Van Santvoord,	Washington, D. C.
Ambrose Wager,	Rhinebeck.
Robert D. Watson,	New York.
John P. Wallace, M. D.	Brooklyn.
Rev. Samuel P. Wells,	Dubuque, Iowa.
Hiram Wheeler,	Claverack.
Henry Wells,	Syracuse.
Francis J. Warner,	Newark, Del.,
Professor in Newark College.	
Archibald Wieting,	Minden.
A. E. Williams, M. D.	Albany.
Rev. John Woodbridge,	Saratoga Springs.
Rev. P. D. Young,	Lansingburgh.

CIII.

1839.

William Allen,	Milwaukee, Wis.
Rev. Charles Anderson,	Union Springs.
Gorham Beales, M. D.	New York City.
L. Lawrence Beebe,	Syracuse.
*Jacques Bennett,	Gravesend.
D. Campbell,	Albany.
M. P. Cavert,	Albany.
Secretary of the Department of Public Instruction.	
Demetrius M. Chadsey,	Schenectady.
Walter Chipman,	Shoreham, Vt.
*William H. Cole,	Lansingburgh.
James H. Cook, M. D.,	Palatine.
Rev. Jonathan Copeland,	Champlain, N. Y.
Rev. Adam Craig,	Windsor.
Uberto Crandal,	Warrensburg.
Caleb B. Crumb,	Rochester.
James Dow,	Richfield.
Rev. James Dunbar,	Northville, Mich.
William E. Eacker,	Spraker's Basin.
James Elmendorf,	Hudson.
Rev. Walter Gunn,	Missionary to China.
*John S. Hannay,	Bern.
Solomon P. Heath,	Amsterdam.
Benjamin M. Hermans,	Saugerties.
Lewis S. Hough,	Valley Bridge, Pa.
*James Houston,	Savannah, Ga.
Rev. James Hoyt,	Hastings, Mich.
Christopher Ives,	Sandlake.
Wynkoop Keirsteed,	Mongaup Valley.
Rufus King,	Davenport.
Rev. Henry M. Lane,	Westfield.
Rev. Saurin E. Lane,	Galway.
Phales Lindsley,	Rushville.
J. G. McChesney,	Schenectady.
Rev. Lawrence Mersereau,	Little Falls.
Joel Miller,	Springfield, Mass.
Thomas C. Miller,	Detroit, Mich.
George D. Moore,	Natches, Miss.
*S. T. Parshall,	Cooperstown.
E. Priest,	Amsterdam.
Rev. Wm. A. Righter,	Newark, N. J.

Rev. P. M. Rightmyer,	Saugerties.
Ansel E. Stephens,	Dayton, Ohio.
Rev. Thomas C. Strong,	Newton, L. I.
David Taylor,	Sheboygan, Wis.
*Rev. J. V. Vandervolger,	Wisconsin.
Rev. Levi F. Waldo,	Poughkeepsie.
Otis F. Waldo,	Milwaukee, Wis.
Rev. Benj. Wells,	Allen.
J. N. Wightman,	Mohawk.
Frederick S. Wood,	Sau River Rapids, Min. Ter.
Rev. Abraham T. Young,	Oaks Corners.
Madison Young,	Fort Desmoines, Iowa.

LII.

1840.

J. S. Chadbourne,	Boston, Mass.
David H. Cruttenden, Principal Mechan's Institute.	New York City,
Charles Davis,	Spencertown.
Rev. Thomas Frazer,	Decatur, Wis.
Samuel H. Furman,	New York.
Rev. Alfred A. Gilbert,	Lanesborough, Mass.
*Ephraim C. Hall,	La Grange.
S. S. Harmon,	California.
Seymour C. Harris,	Fabius.
Rev. M. S. Ingersol,	Newark, N. J.
Rev. Joshua Kennedy,	Conecocheque, Pa.
Oscar F. Knox,	Augusta, Ga.
Rev. A. M. McChesney,	Lexington, Ky.
Rev. Wm. S. McLaren,	Caledonia.
Rev. C. D. McVain,	Franklinville.
John R. Miller,	Norwich, Mass.
Peter S. Nellis,	Palatine.
J. A. Northrop,	Spencertown.
Rev. J. Jermaine Porter,	Watertown.
Aaron Potter,	Albion, Mich.
Wm. S. Robertson,	Creek Mission, Mich.
Henry M. Robertson,	Neenah, Wis.
Rev. Rodman H. Robinson,	West Troy.
Rev. Erastus Ripley,	Davenport, Iowa.
Benjamin B. Smith,	Jonesdale.
Samuel S. Stafford,	Albany.
*R. T. Talman,	Schenectady.

XXVII.

1845.

Wm. L. Akin,	New York.
Ephraim R. Akin, M. D.,	McGranville.
Jesse Andrews,	Natches, Miss.
Rev. H. A. Austin,	Worthington, Mass.
S. J. Austin,	Waterford, Va.
Rev. John Bannard,	Crescent.
Arie Banta,	Washara, Wis.
Daniel R. Bigelow,	Mineral Point, Ill.
Rev. Alfred P. Bottsford,	Red Mills.
Warren G. Brown,	Albany.
Duncan E. Cameron,	Milwaukee, Wis.
Rev. William N. Calderwood,	Missionary to India.
John Carmichael,	West Galway.
Rev. James S. Cowper,	Scotland.
Aaron S. Cronkite,	Neenah, Wis.
James Darrow,	Denmark.
Rev. Alexander Dickson,	Albany.
James S. Dobbin,	Salem.
*H. Woodward Freeman,	Saratoga Springs.
Hiram N. Gates,	Yankee Settlement, Ia.
Elias Hand,	Elkhorn, Wis.
Rev. Luther B. Hart,	Norfolk, Ct.
George H. Hearman,	Troy.
Rev. Francis Hendricks,	Philadelphia, Pa.
Wm. C. Hickox,	Montrose, Pa.
S. Marshall Ingalls,	Canajoharie.
Charles J. King,	Freehold.
*Lauren Kellogg,	Amsterdam.
Rev. Nathaniel B. Klink,	Ballston.
Rev. Julian Lansing,	Missionary to Turkey.
Rev. David B. Lyon,	———, Wis.
Rev. Wm. J. Magill,	Canonsburg, Pa.
Rev. Joseph McCracken,	York.
Rev. Wm. Milroy,	Miami, Ohio.
Byron Mix,	New York.
*Finley McKercher,	York.
Rev. Peter D. McNab,	York.
Charles C. Nott,	New York.
Rev. John W. Nott,	Fustburg.
D. C. Nichols,	Chicago, Ill.
Rev. Richard Osborn,	Champion.

RANSOM R. PECK, Farmerville.
Rev. JEREMIAH PETRIE, Volney.
Rev. BRADLEY PHILLIPS, Honkon, Wis.
*B. F. RAPPELYE, Farmerville.
ROBERT ROGERS, Charlotteville.
ALBERT Y. SCHERMERHORN, M. D., Glens Falls.
M. J. SHOECRAFT, Oneida Depot.
Rev. AMOS H. SILL, Mareau.
Rev. WILLIAM C. SOMERS, Cuilerville.
CHARLES M. TALLMAN, Albany.
LEWIS TICE, M. D. Meridian.
Rev. RANSOM B. WELCH, Oswego.
D. P. WHEDON, New York.
A. M. WILLIAMS, M. D., Manlius.
ROSWELL A. WYMAN, Parma.

LVI.

1846.

Rev. THOMAS E. BLISS, North Middleboro.
ELI C. BOTTSFORD, Yorkville.
*REUBEN L. BOYNTON, Owasco.
Rev. LAWRENCE L. COMFORT, Whitehouse, N. J.
DANIEL J. DARROW, Schenectady.
EDWARD C. DODGE, Jordan.
STEPHEN FRADENBURGH, Mareau.
*Rev. GEORGE FURBECK, Guilderland.
WILLIAM T. GOODNOUGH, Theresa.
Rev. ROBERT GRAY, Newark, N. J.
THEODORE HYATT, Wilmington, Del.
JOSEPH W. HUNSICKER, Norristown, Pa.
CHARLES J. LANSING, Lansingburgh.
GEORGE H. MANN, Buenos Ayres, S. A.
JOHN A. McFARLAND, Salem.
Rev. GEORGE McQUEEN, Jr., Missionary to Africa.
ABEL MERCHANT, Nassau.
WILLIAM C. ROGERS, M. D. Schenectady.
GARDNER R. SCRIVEN, New York.
Rev. NICHOLAS J. SEELEY, Burnt Hills.
Rev. JAMES M. SMEALLIE, Birmingham, Mich.
SILAS SMITH, Half Moon.
Rev. WICKS S. TITUS, Pennington, N. J.
SAMUEL M. TRACY, St. Anthony's Falls, Min.
Rev. DAVID TULLY, Ballston.
CORNELIUS J. VANDERBILT, New York City.

XXVII.

1847.

E. W. Beebe,	Leicester.
Rev. Rabbi J. W. Buckland,	New York City.
Rev. Henry B. Burr,	———.
Rev. Robert Crookshank,	Bellport, L. I.
Rev. James Crookshank,	Ogdensburgh.
Jacob B. Decker,	Red Creek.
John Edgar,	Newburg.
Henry Gardner,	Albany.
Rev. Andrew Gordon,	Missionary to Sand. Is.
Rev. Joel Huntington,	Milwaukee, Wis.
John A. King,	New York.
Sanford B. Kinney,	Scott.
Henry A. Lounsbury,	Auburn.
T. Willard Lewis,	South Royalston, Mass.
Rev. A. McWilliam,	Pine Bush.
J. Clemens Miller,	Phœnixville, Pa.
W. Irving Pond,	Alexandria, D. C.
Charles Putnam,	Hamlin.
Rev. David H. Thayer,	Hamden, Ct.
Joseph M. Wilkin,	Nashville, Tenn.

XX.

1848.

John C. Bishop,	Spencertown.
Nathaniel Merritt,	Seneca Falls.
Rev. Stephen Searle,	N. B. Theo. Seminary.
Rev. Charles S. Vedder,	Schenectady,
Tutor, Union College.	
R. Howard Wallace,	Little Britain.

V.

1849.

*Samuel Barkley,	West Hebron.
Spencer J. Fowler,	Kingsville, O.
Jacob Fry,	Geddesburg, O.
Edwin D. Helms,	St. Louis, Mo.
G. M. Livingston,	Johnstown.
Rev. Andrew McIntyre,	Lewiston.
J. J. P. Ostrander,	Philadelphia, Pa.
Hermon Perry,	Wyoming.
Rev. William C. Phillips,	Burnt Hill.
James H. Vail,	St. Louis, Mo.
James S. Warner,	St. Louis, Mo.
Rev. John Williams, Jr.,	Marion, O.
*Joshua K. Yeakle,	Hereford, Pa.

XIII.

1850.

Daniel F. Akin,	Pittstown.
Wm. Currie,	Newburg.
George M. Howe,	Sudbury, Mass.
William J. Johnson,	———, Ill.
George W. Righter,	Conshohocken, Pa.
Ambrose C. Spicer,	Janesville, Ill.
John L. Thompson,	Bloomingrove.
Wm. C. Whitford,	New York.
Rev. Franklin D. Wright,	Moravia.

IX.

1851.

Rev. Edward L. Bailey,	Carbondale, Pa.
John J. Cameron,	Princeton Theo. Seminary.
Rev. Luman B. Chamberlain,	Woodstock, Pa.
Orlow W. Chapman,	Ellington, Ct.
Phillip Furbeck,	N. B. Theo. Seminary.
Peter R. Furbeck,	Schenectady.
John G. Gray,	New Orleans, La.
John Harper,	Xenia Theological Sem.
David Herron, Jr.,	Troy.
Robert Hood,	Elmira.
John Kehoo,	Princeton Theo. Seminary.
Abraham G. Lansing,	Choctaw Nation.
James C. Laverty,	Philadelphia, Pa.
James McArthur,	Xenia Theo. Seminary.
George Marshall,	Princeton Theo. Seminary.
Herman H. Pierce,	East Davenport.
Hiram Scofield,	Cambridge.
Peter Smeallie,	Johnston.
Andrew J. Southwick,	Easton.
*Rev. Horace Stone,	Warren, Mass.
Carlos Swift,	Fabius.
Alvah Traver,	Sandlake.

XXII.

1852.

Alexander Adair,	Newbury Theo. Seminary.
Joseph L. Clark,	Newbury Theo. Seminary.
John Gibson,	Ryegate, Vt.
Wolcott N. Griswold,	Albany.
Nathaniel P. Henderson,	New Hamburg.
Alfred Milmine,	Florida.
Charles C. Miller,	Geneseo.
John H. Miller,	Lyonier, Pa.

Alexander J. Robb,	Florida.
Andrew J. Rodman,	Summit.
Henry B. Thayer,	Cohoes.
Philo G. Valentine,	Slaterville.
Roswell D. Valentine,	Slaterville.
Albert Woodcock,	Fitz Henry, Ill.
Albert L. York,	Brookfield.

XV.

1853.

Ormanzo Allen,	Milton, Wis.
Henry D. Burlingham,	South Hartford.
*Ethan Clark,	Ovid.
Amos R. Cornwell,	Alfred.
William G. Donnan,	Rockville, Ia.
William H. Essex,	Oswego.
William Wallace Kirby,	Roslyn, L. I.
P. Miller,	———.
*Adam Van Vanken,	Clifton Park.
Edward A. Warriner,	West Springfield, Mass.

X.

1854.

F. A. Chase,	Genoa.
John Cromlish,	Pittsburgh, Pa.
E. H. Davis,	Shiloh, N. J.
Wm. F. Freeman,	Stillwater.
Alexander Hadden,	Montgomery.
Lemuel E. Heritage,	Shiloh, N. J.
S. A. Knapp,	Coxsackie.
A. B. McClelland,	Cambridge.
Marcus P. Norton,	Tinmouth, Vt.
E. H. Peterson,	Nunda.
William H. Silvernail,	Chatham.
James Wilkinson,	Pottsdam.
William A. Wilson,	Chartier Valley, Pa.
Thomas C. Woodward,	Marlboro, Pa.

XIV.

1855.

C. B. Allen,	Auburn.
*Harlow Bowman,	Canajoharie.
Sydney R. Burnap,	Charleston.
Henry A. Buttz,	Coolbaughs, Pa.
Charles H. Chapman,	Northumberland.
Robert Denniston, Jr.,	Salisbury Mills.
J. B. Emins,	Hammond.

Fredrrick W. Flint,	Fayetteville.
Philip K. Gleed,	Waterville, Vt.
Joseph Graham,	Nilna.
Henry L. Harter,	Jordanville.
Jesse M. Holmes,	Hammond.
George W. Hough,	Waterloo.
Isaac H. Kirby,	Roslyn, L. I.
Thomas Lallout,	Charlotteville.
W. Lallout,	Wyoming, Pa.
J. B. McChesney,	Scaghticoke.
Adiel S. Morse,	Watertown.
Thomas A. Samson,	Princeton.
Charles P. Shaw,	Jay.
Chester C. Thorne,	Laurens.
George E. Tomlinson,	Adams Center.
Horace T. S. Tupper,	Moresville.
F. V. Van Vanken,	Princeton.
Warren Wilkie,	Re Roy.

XXV.

1856.

Lucien E. Carter,	Carthage, N. Y.
Don Alonzo Hulett,	Henvelton, N. Y.
Hiram C. Johns,	Mainsburg, Pa.
A. W. Miller,	Governeur, N. Y.
N. L. Snow,	Root, N. Y.
Henry L. Warner,	Howard, Mass.
Oscar F. Whitford,	Northumberland.

VII.

1857.

J. Henry Becker,	Saratoga, N. Y.

I.

1858.

Edwin R. Beach,	Liberty, N. Y.
A. J. Blakely,	Pawlet, Vt.
Collins Blakely,	Pawlet, Vt.
S. E. Blakely,	Pawlet, Vt.
Jno. P. Buckley,	Freeport, Pa.
J. B. Burt,	Dubuque, Iowa.
J. T. Butts,	Clarksville, N. Y.
John H. Carter,	New Milford, Ct.
John G. Everts,	Havana, N. Y.
G. W. Fitch,	Cambridge, N. Y.
Ethan A. Ives,	Norway, N. Y.

J. W. Johnson,	Stewiacke, Nova Scotia.
Wm. H. Pitt,	Granger, N. Y.
James S. Smart,	Cambridge, N. Y.
S. M. Thorp,	Granger, N. Y.
Thomas J. Thorp,	Granger, N. Y.
Benjamin A. Willis,	Roslyn, L. I.
Wm. T. Willis,	Alden, N. Y.
	XVIII.

1859.

M. H. Close,	Covert. N. Y.
J. M. Hartwell,	Charlotteville, N. Y.
	II.

1862.

Charles M. Carter,	Ballston.
George W. Fitch,	Cambridge.
James W. Johnston,	Stewiacke, Nova Scotia.
David N. Lewis,	Wells, Vt.
Henry E. Ogden,	Walton.
Charles Styre,	Norristown, Pa.
Samuel Yeoman,	Franklin.
John D. Young,	Springfield.
	VIII.

863.

A. Watson Atwood,	Philadelphia, Pa.
G. Arnotte Beattie,	Hebron.
Daniel Bosworth,	Baltimore, Md.
James Yates,	Chicago, Ill.
	IV.

1864.

A. D. Fessenden,	Townsend.
	I.

1865.

Edmond T. Davis,	Shiloh, N. J.
JOHN V. GRISWOLD,	Quincy, Ill.
	II.

Amherst Chapter.

Founded in 1847.

MEMBERS.

Names.	*Class.*	*Residences.*
	1848.	
Rev. IRA CASE,		Underhill, Vt.
Rev. WM. A. FOBES,		West Lebanon, Me.
Rev. MARTIN L. GAYLORD,		———.
MIRON J. HAZELTINE,		Lowell.
Rev. ROBERT D. MILLER,		North Wardsboro, Vt.
Rev. JOHN Q. PEABODY,		Fryeburgh, Me.
HIRAM A. PRATT,		Suffield, Ct.
		VII.
	1849.	
*GEORGE W. CURRIER,		West Boylston.
Rev. DANIEL F. GODDARD,		Boston.
Rev. CHARLES HARTWELL,		Fuh Chau, China.
Rev. JUNIUS L. HATCH,		Brooklyn, N. Y.
*Rev. HUBERT P. HERRICK,		Gaboon Mission, Africa.
ELIJAH HOWE, Jr.,		Boston.
Rev. WM. R. PALMER,		Attica, Ind.
MARTIN N. ROOT, M. D.,		Francistown, N. H.
Rev. JOHN A. SEYMOUR,		South Glastenbury, Ct.
Rev. GEORGE I. STEARNS,		Windham, Ct.
Rev. ELIJAH W. STODDARD,		Succasunna, N. J.
GEORGE F. WALKER,		Holliston.
		XII.

1850.

Rev. Albert G. Beebe,	Manitowoc, Wis.
Rev. John E. Cory,	Chesterfield.
Rev. Daniel W. Faunce,	Worcester.
Sidney S. Merrill, M. D.,	San Francisco, Cal.
Ira L. Moore, M. D.,	Lowell.
	V.

1851.

*Rev. Henry M. Adams,	Gaboon Mission, Africa.
Jerome Allen,	Dubuque, Ia.,
Professor of Chemistry and Botany,	Alexander College.
Rev. Wm. O. Baldwin,	Hana Mission, Sand. Is.
Edward P. Bates,	West Cambridge.
Rev. Marcus M. Carleton,	Amoy, China.
Rev. Isaac N. Cundall,	Rosendale, Wis.
Rev. Franklin B. Doe,	Lancaster.
Rev. Eben. Douglass, Jr.,	Oldtown, Me.
Rev. Francis A. Douglass,	Nellore, India.
Rev. Prescott Fay,	Lancaster, N. H.
Rev. Levi G. Marsh,	Nunda, N. Y.
Rev. Hugh McLeod,	Brentwood, N. H.
Sidney K. B. Perkins,	Braintree.
Edward D. Rawson,	——, Pa.
	XIV.

1852.

Rev. Osborn P. Allen,	Karpoot, W. Asia.
Rev. Geo. L. Becker,	Sandford, Me.
Rev. Daniel Bliss,	Abeih, Syria.
Joseph M. Clark, M. D.,	Metamora, Ill.
Rev. Elijah S. Fish,	Freeport, Me.
Buel J. Hawkins,	Conneaut, O.
*Henry Kies,	Troy, Ia.
Fayette Maynard,	Potsdam, N. Y.
Mason Moore,	Fredonia, N. Y.
Charles H. Payson,	New York City.
Charles L. Porter,	Prattsburg, N. Y.
William B. Rankin,	Greenville, Tenn.,
President of Greenville	College.
Sydney K. Smith,	Columbia, S. C.
	XIII.

1853.

Thomas D. Adams,	Framingham.

Robert C. Allison,	Salina, Pa.
Rev. Nathaniel B. Blanchard,	Plymouth.
James Buckland,	St. Louis, Mo.
Rev. George W. Clark,	Newmarket, N. J.
Rev. Amos H. Coolidge,	Leicester.
Rev. Samuel C. Dean,	Seroor, India.
Enoch K. Evans,	———.
Rev. Joseph L. A. Fish,	Webster.
Rev. William D. Flagg,	Barton, Vt.
James R. Hale,	Canton, N. Y.
Rev. Daniel C. Litchfield,	Bowdoinham, Me.
Rev. Charles F. Morse,	Adrianople, W. Asia.
Ralph L. Parsons, M. D.,	Blackwell's Island, N. Y.
Elbridge Pepper,	Newton Theo. Seminary.
Henry R. Pierce,	Uxbridge.
Edward H. Pratt,	East Woodstock, Ct.
Rev. Gilbert B. Richardson,	Douglass Centre.
Rev. Geo. E. Sanborne,	Georgia, Vt.
Julius Spencer,	Princeton Theo. Seminary.
Sanborn Tenney,	Auburndale,
Lecturer before Massachusetts Teachers' Institute.	
Abner H. Wenzell,	Pittsburgh, Pa.

XXII.

1854.

Rev. Israel Brundage,	Prompton, Pa.
Edwin Cooley,	Marion, Ia.,
State Geological Surveyor.	
Rev. Edwin Dimock,	Orange,
Tutor in Amherst College.	
Henry C. Fay,	———.
Heman M. Glass,	Lime, N. Y.
Adoniram J. Goodnough,	Medical College, Boston.
George D. A. Hebard,	———, Ia.
Rev. Milan H. Hitchcock,	Manepy, India.
Rev. Charles H. Hollaway,	Middletown, Del.
Franklin Hubbard,	Adrian, Mich.
Charles A. Kimball,	Ipswich.
John C. Kimball,	DivinitySchool,Camb'dge,
Professor in Marshall University.	
Willard Merrill,	Prairie Du Chien, Wis.
Norman A. Prentiss,	Danville, Ill.
Charles P. Rugg,	Fairhaven.

Uriel W. Small,	Andover.
*Silas M. Smith,	Waterloo, N. Y.

XVII.

1855.

Eli G. Bennett,	Brooklyn, N. Y.
Albert H. Bridgman,	Maysville, Ia.
Francis F. Brown,	Sudbury.
John C. Caldwell,	East Machias, Me.
Micah S. Croswell,	Geneseo, Ill.
Charles H. Crowell,	Windham, N. H.
James W. Crowell,	Londonderry, N. H.
Appleton H. Fitch,	Dover, N. H.
John Hartwell,	East Windsor Theo. Sem.
Rev. Martin S. Howard,	Pelham.
Savilian R. Hull,	Cheshire, Ct.
Rev. Chester B. Jefferds,	Chester, Vt.
J. Brown Lord,	Cambridge Law School.
William L. Montague,	Amherst,
Instructor in Latin and French, Amherst College.	
Moses Noerr,	Princeton Theo. Seminary.
Levi S. Packard,	Chatham, N. Y.
Henry J. Richardson,	Topsfield.
Horace L. Singleton,	Princeton Theo. Seminary.
Ezra T. Sprague,	Madison, Wis.
Rev. George Washburn,	Constantinople, Turkey.

XX.

1856.

Lyman Bartlett,	East Windsor Theo. Sem.
James A. Bates,	Andover Theo. Seminary.
Josiah Beardsley,	Ellsworth, O.
*Rev. Joseph Bloomer,	McGregor's, Ia.
William F. Bradbury,	Cambridge.
Edward E. Bradbury,	Brooklyn, N. Y.
Chester Brigham,	Princeton Theo. Seminary.
Chester L. Cushman,	South Danvers.
Josiah H. Goddard,	———, Ill.
Edward P. Goodwin,	Union Theo. Sem., N. Y.
Charles E. Griggs,	Union Theo. Sem., N. Y.
George M. Guernsey,	Owego, N. Y.
Hiram C. Hayd'n,	Union Theo. Sem., N. Y.
Thomas P. Herrick,	Canandaigua, N. Y.
*James E. Hutchinson,	Jacksonville, Pa.

Edward P. Kimball,	Ipswich.
*Frederick W. Lane,	North Brookfield.
John W. Lane,	Andover Theo. Seminary.
Joel Linsly,	Millville, N. Y.
Benjamin Mattice,	Belle Plain, Minn.
Franklin B. Norton,	Worcester.
Cyrus H. Pendleton,	Bozrah, Ct.
Nathan C. Pond,	East Brookfield.
Martin L. Richardson,	Bangor Theo. Seminary.
James Russell,	Winchester.
Joseph Russell,	———, Ala.
William Swinton,	Montreal, L. C.

XXVII.

1857.

Charles E. Allen,	Princeton.
Henry F. Blodgett,	Stafford, Ct.
J. Theodore Briggs,	Orange.
Wm. O. Carr,	Andover Theo. Seminary.
Jacob C. Clapp,	Newton, N. C.
Asahel L. Clark,	Hyde Park, Pa.
George T. Higley,	Ashland.
Henry W. Jones,	East Windsor Theo. Sem.
Daniel W. Richardson,	Middleton.
Daniel H. Rogan,	Auburn Theo. Seminary.
Daniel F. Savage,	Andover Theo. Seminary.
Abiel H. Slayton,	Woodstock, Vt.
Denis Wortman, Jr.,	N.BrunswickTh.Sem.,N.J.

XIII.

1858.

James B. Beaumont,	Canandaigua, N. Y.
Daniel Bliss,	Andover Theo. Seminary.
William L. Bray,	Con.Theo.Sem.Chicago,Ill.
Andrew J. Clapp,	Andover Theo. Seminary.
George C. Clarke,	Con.Theo.Sem.Chicago,Ill.
Royal W. Clark,	Union Theo. Seminary.
James Collins,	Pineville, Pa.
Edward P. Gardner,	Buffalo, N. Y.
Stephen Harris,	East Windsor Theo. Sem.
Henry Hastings,	Union Theo. Seminary.
Chester W. Hawley,	Waterville, N. Y.
Edwin Hunt,	Sudbury.
Henry M. Kellogg,	Shelburne.

Edwin E. Merriam,	Sunsbury, N. C.
George H. Miles,	Rutland.
Samuel B. Sherrill,	Andover Theo. Seminary.
Havilah M. Sprague,	New York City.
Gardner P. Stickney,	Andover Theo. Seminary.
James E. Tower,	North Hadley.
Justin E. Twichell,	Xenia, O.
John Whitehall,	Andover Theo. Seminary.
Charles B. Whittlesey,	Berlin, Ct.
James D. Wilson,	Spring Mills, Pa.

XXIII.

1859.

Sanford Waters Billings,	Sharon.
Henry J. Bruce,	Springfield.
George Constantine,	Athens, Greece.
John F. Gleason,	Bedford.
Samuel E. Herrick,	Southampton, N. Y.
Luther Keene, Jr.,	Atkinson, Me.
Frederic W. Pike,	Mercer, Me.
*Willard J. Putnam,	Hopkinton.
Philander Read,	Wattsburgh, Pa.
Amos F. Shattuck,	Hollis, N. H.
Henry M. Stevens,	Bluehill, Me.
Wesley Squier,	Wales.
James N. Thresher,	Stafford, Ct.
J. Osmand Tiffany,	Attleboro'.
Henry Tupper,	Monson.

XV.

1860.

Henry E. Barnes,	Plantsville, Ct.
William Brown,	Concord.
Horace Cannon,	Wareham.
George Curtiss,	Union, Ct.
George Dexter,	Worcester.
Lucius H. Higgins,	Plantsville, Ct.
Clinton M. Jones,	Bangor, Me.
George A. Keene,	Atkinson, Me.
Joseph Mason,	Attleboro'.
Lucius L. Merrick,	Palmer.
Horace Parker,	Milford.
Willard Putnam,	New Salem.
S. John Storrs,	Amherst.

EDWARD R. WHEELER, Spencer.

XIV.

1861.

FRANCIS H. BOYNTON, Amherst.
WILLIAM J. CLARK, St. Louis, Mo.
FRANKLIN C. FLINT, Shrewsbury.
JAMES LAIRD, Clinton.
GEORGE F. MERRIAM, Temple, N. H.
DAVID S. MORGAN, Andover.
DANIEL T. NELSON, Milford.
M. PORTER SNELL, North Brookfield.

VIII.

1862.

BENJAMIN A. DEAN, Shrewsbury.
HENRY A. FORD, Lacon, Ill.
JOHN GODDARD, North Bridgewater.
HERVEY C. HAZEN, Ithaca, N. Y.
EBEN POPE, Dorchester.

V.

Hamilton Chapter.

Founded in 1847.

MEMBERS.

Names.	*Class.*	*Residences.*
Rev. Albert Barnes,		Philadelphia, Pa.
Rev. William S. Curtis, President of Knox College.		Galesburg, Ill.,
Rev. L. Merril Miller,		Ogdensburg, N. Y.
Rev. Henry A. Nelson,		St. Louis, Mo.
Rev. Joel Parker,		Newark, N. J.
Prof. H. H. Sanford,		Homer, N. Y.
		VI.
	1848.	
*Rev. Augustus G. Gould,		Cortlandville, N. Y.
Rev. Richard G. Keyes,		Watertown, N. Y.
George R. Martin,		Fredonia, N. Y.
Rev. Stewart Sheldon,		Wellsville, N. Y.
Rev. Milton Waldo,		Hornellsville, N. Y.
		V.
	1849.	
Rev. David E. Blain,		Puget's Sound, Oregon.
Rev. John Campbell,		Johnstonville, O.
Rev. Yates Hickey,		Greenville, N. Y.
Rev. Hiram E. Johnson,		Dennisville, N. J.
Henry C. Kingsbury,		Westfield, N. Y.
George W. Newcomb,		Chicago, Ill.
Ellison Robbins,		Santa Clara, Cal.
Rev. Alfred M. Stowe,		Canandaigua, N. Y.
Rev. Alvin D. Williams,		Minneapolis, Min.
		IX.

1850.

IRA W. ALLEN,	Yellow Springs, O.,
Professor of Mathematics, Antioch College.	
*LE ROY BLISS,	West Winfield, N. Y.
Rev. BYRON BOSWORTH,	Henrietta, N. Y.
Rev. GILES B. CLEVELAND,	Philadelphia, Pa.
GUY K. CLEVELAND,	Mankato, Wis.
SAMUEL S. CAMP,	Laurens, N. Y.
JAMES CONVERSE,	Woodville, N. Y.
Rev. LAURENTINE HAMILTON,	Oakland, Cal.
EDWARD O. HAMLIN,	Wilkesbarre, Pa.
CHARLES H. MEIGS,	Binghamton, N. Y.
M. TOWNLEY TUTHILL,	Utica.
Rev. WARREN W. WARNER,	Jefferson.

XII.

1851.

EGBERT L. BANGS,	Flint, Mich.
Professor of Deaf and Dumb Asylum.	
GEORGE L. BROCKETT,	Flint, Mich.
Professor of Deaf and Dumb Asylum.	
Rev. EDWIN R. DAVIS,	West Avon.
THOMAS EVANS,	Plainfield, Ind.
Rev. FRANCIS F. FORD,	Kalamazoo, Mich.
JOSEPH C. FORD,	Madison, Wis.
SETH E. HILLS,	Fond Du Lac, Wis.
LOUIS H. JENKINS,	Jacksonville, Ill.,
Professor of Deaf and Dumb Asylum.	
DANIEL J. PRATT,	Albany, N. Y.
HIRAM L. WARD,	Aurora, N. Y.

X.

1852.

*HENRY B. BOYNTON,	Cahawba, Ala.
Rev. EDWIN O. BURNHAM,	———, Mich.
JOHN C. DONALDSON,	Butternuts, N. Y.
ROSWELL H. KINNEY,	Columbus, O.
Rev. WM. J. KNOX,	Augusta, N. Y.
JABEZ R. WARD,	Minneapolis, Minn.
HENRY S. WELTON,	Iowa City, Ia.,
Professor of Languages, Iowa College.	

VII.

1853.

JOHN M. BRAYTON,	Delhi, Ia.
*THEODORE W. BURNETT,	Cape Vincent, N. Y.
Rev. WM. B. DADA,	Minneapolis, Minn.
SIMEON HACKLEY,	Oakala, Ill.

Rev. Alexander McLean,	———, Ct.
Edward De Roy Stark,	Whitestown, N. Y.
Rev. Alanson Tilden,	Troupsburgh, N. Y.
Joseph S. Winans,	Sidney Center, N. Y.
	VIII.

1854.

*Charles Baylies,	Clinton, N. Y.
Rev. Wm. H. Maynard,	Cohoes, N. Y.
George S. Morse,	Columbia, Mo.
Rev. Wm. L. Page,	Wolcott, N. Y.
*Wm. Richmond,	Lee, N. Y.
Rev. Dwight T. Scovel,	Lakeville.
	VI.

1855.

Rev. Nelson N. Avery,	Flushing, N. Y.
Milton T. Hills,	Nunda, N. Y.
Rev. John F. Kendall,	Baldwinsville, N. Y.
Joel M. Manwaring,	Sidney Center, N. Y.
	IV.

1856.

Truman G. Avery,	Buffalo.
*Theodore Beard,	Pompey, N. Y.
Rev. Alphonso L. Benton,	Lima.
Rev. Wm. J. Erdman,	Fayetteville, N. Y.
William C. Gray,	Moreland, N. Y.
Milton Howe,	Phelps, N. Y.
George C. Pattison,	Natchez, Miss.
Rev. Archibald M. Shaw,	Constantia.
Rev. Charles E. Stebbins,	Ovid.
	IX.

1857.

James S. Baker,	New York City.
Rev. John H. Dillingham,	Winona, Ill.
*Duncan McArthur Parker,	New York City.
Rev. Arthur Tappan Pierson,	Waterford, N. Y.
Walter Smith,	Clinton.
Rev. Joseph E. Tinker,	Willoughby, O.
	VI.

1858.

Edward P. Adams,	Auburn.
Cyrus C. Camp,	Troy, Kansas.
*Samuel Camp,	Clinton, N. Y.
Rev. Albert Erdman,	Clinton, N. Y.
Charles H. Hamlin,	Buffalo, N. Y.
	V.

1859.

Rev. Alvin Baker,	Norwalk, Ct.
Norton W. Boomer,	Whitesboro, N. Y.
George W. Kellogg,	Clinton, N. Y.
Rev. Delevan L. Leonard,	New Preston, Ct.
Rev. Leicester J. Sawyer,	Whitesboro, N. Y.
Rev. Wm. A. Wolcott,	Campbell.
	VI.

1860.

Rev. Samuel Miller,	Eaton, N. Y.
Rev. Theodore S. Pond,	New York City.
Rev. Isaac P. Powell,	Clinton, N. Y.
*Rev. Comfort Israel Slack,	Newton, Iowa.
Rev. Samuel D. Westfall,	Lyons.
	V.

1861.

Porter C. Bliss,	Brazil, S. A.
Albert L. Childs,	Waterloo, N. Y.
J. Sandford Greves,	New York City.
D. L. Kiehle.	Preston, Minn.
Wm. H. H. Miller,	Fort Wayne, Ind.
George J. North,	Des Moines, Ia.
Francis A. Torrey,	Vernon, N. Y.
Rev. William W. Wetmore,	Des Moines, Ia.
	IX.

1862.

J. Newton Beach,	Watkins.
Norman H. Becker,	Seneca Falls.
Seymour H. Dibble,	San Francisco, Cal.
J. Q. A. Hollister,	Westfield, N. Y.
Horace H. Hollister,	East Pembroke, N. Y.
John McLean,	Galena, Ill.
Levi D. Miller,	Little Falls, N. Y.
J. Robert Moore,	Trenton Falls, N. Y.
*Lansford S. Page,	Sangerfield, N. Y.
*J. J. Pease,	Floyd, N. Y.
L. S. B. Sawyer,	Schoharie, N. Y.
Henry Ward,	Auburn Theo. Sem.
Henry Ward, Jr.,	La Fargeville, N. Y.
	XIII.

1863.

Myron Adams, Jr.,	Auburn Theo. Sem.
*Henry P. Cook,	Dundee, N. Y.
Killed at the Battle of Gettysburg.	
P. Q. Eckerson,	Seneca Falls, N. Y.

*G. A. Markham,	Lee Centre, N. Y.
*Geo. W. Sheldon,	West Bloomfield, N. Y.
J. Seymour Slie,	Wolcott, N. Y.
Augustus B. Southwick,	Rome, N. Y.
	VII.

1864.

Rev. Geo. Bayless,	Phelps, N. Y.
Theo. F. Jessup,	Florida, N. Y.
Henry Leutsinger,	Princeton, N. J.
Henry Loomis,	Auburn Theo. Sem.
*Norman C. McMath,	Webster, N. Y.
*Alfred A. Morse,	Eaton, N. Y.
Kendrick S. Putnam,	Rome, N. Y.
Darius C. Sackett,	Auburn Theo. Sem.
Justin Smith, Jr.,	Mt. Morris, N. Y.
*Mason C. Smith,	Perry, N. Y.
Geo. Galitzin Truair,	Syracuse.
*Geo. A. Watson,	Fredonia, N. Y.
Killed at the Battle of Black Water.	
Chas. Henry West, Jr.,	Medina, N. Y.
*Albert P. Worthington,	Vineland, N. J.
	XIV.

1865.

William Henry Bates,	Auburn Theo. Sem.
Oscar H. Elmer,	Union Theo. Sem.
Jas. A. Ferguson,	Ogdensburg, N. Y.
Henry Foord,	Cazenovia, N. Y.
Jas. P. Kimball,	Berkshire, N. Y.
Geo. W. Martin,	Union Theo. Sem.
Luther A. Ostrander,	Constantinople, Turkey.
James Rodgers,	Constantinople, Turkey.
Jas. P. Stratton,	Philadelphia, Pa.
	IX.

1866.

Joseph Y. Chapin,	Ogdensburg, N. Y.
George Norton,	Chatanooga, Tenn.
E. R. Payson,	Oxford, N. Y.
Chas. Simpson,	Peekskill.
S. Darwin Wilcox,	Cortlandville.
	V.

1867.

James B. Avery,	Oneida Castle, N. Y.
Isaac O. Best,	Ogdensburg, N. Y.
J. Earl Hall,	Argyle, N. Y.

Martin F. Hollister,	Ithaca, N. Y.
Chas. E. Rice,	Fairfield, N. Y.
Samuel Wm. Wetzel,	Utica, N. Y.
	VI.

1868.

Charles B. Austin,	Philadelphia, Pa.
Otis J. Eddy,	Brooklyn, N. Y.
Cassius H. Dibble,	East Bloomfield, N. Y.
Edwin M. Nelson,	St. Louis, Mo.
Henry N. Payne,	Janesville, Wis.
Louis D. Pomeroy,	Ogdensburgh, N. Y.
Henry R. Waite,	Carthage, N. Y.
Myron G. Willard,	Holland Patent, N. Y.
	VIII.

1869.

Francis M. Burdick,	De Ruyter, N. Y.
William L. Downing,	Oneida, N. Y.
John E. Elmer,	Chester, N. Y.
DeLinton W. Greenfield,	Rome, N. Y.
Martin D. Kneeland,	South Onondaga, N. Y.
Willard M. Lillibridge,	Holland Patent, N. Y.
Charles H. Searle,	Leonardsville, N. Y.
George R. Smith,	Albion, N. Y.
Selden H. Talcott,	Rome, N. Y.
	IX.

1870.

Edward W. Abbey,	Watkins,N. Y.
L. Brainerd Clark,	Clark's Mills, N. Y.
Delos E. Finks,	New Berlin, N. Y.
Sylvester Gardner,	Fayetteville, N. Y.
Fred. H. Gouge,	Trenton, N. Y.
Henry C. Maine,	De Ruyter, N. Y.
Homer W. Searle,	Leonardsville, N. Y.
Sheldon W. Swaney,	Syracuse, N. Y.
	VIII.

Waterville Chapter.

Founded in 1850.

MEMBERS.

Names.	*Class.*	*Residences.*
	1852.	
George W. Dow,		Boston, Mass.
Ebenezer H. Libby,		Wayne.
Rev. George M. Preston,		Medford, Mass.
Daniel W. Wilcox,		Shelburne Falls, Mass.
		IV.
	1853.	
Osborn P. Bigelow,		Boston, Mass.
John A. Lowell,		Lewiston.
Joshua W. Weston,		Skowhegan.
		III.
	1854.	
Albion K. P. Knowlton,		Thomaston.
		I.
	1855.	
James T. Bradbury,		Waterville.
Linton C. Cornforth,		Waterville.
David F. Crane,		Boston, Mass.
Peleg S. Haskell,		Hartland.
*Washington I. Humphrey,		Yarmouth.
John W. Lamb,		Lebanon.
Charles F. Richards,		Lincolnville.
L. Richmond Webber,		Vassalboro'.
		VIII.
	1856.	
Columbus Cornforth,		Waterville.
A. Robinson Crane,		Fayette.
Frederick B. Dunton,		Lincolnville.

Andrew J. Lang,	Fort Plain, N. Y.
Charles C. Low,	Waterville.
Asa Perkins, Jr.,	Thomaston.
Isaac Powers,	Norridgewock.
Joseph A. Ross,	Nobleboro'.
Roscoe G. Smith,	New Hampton, N. H.
Rev. Albion P. Tracy,	Montville.
	X.

1857.

*John B. Bradbury,	Limington.
Wm. J. Corthell,	Calais.
J. Murray Drake,	Sharon, Mass.
Augustus A. Fletcher,	Oldtown.
Jonathan S. Houghton,	Anson.
Rev. George M. P. King,	Farmington.
Francis Mayo,	Georgetown, Ill.
Frank L. Morse,	Glasgow, Ky.
Joseph Odell,	Lebanon, Ky.
Moses J. Prescott,	Ipswich, Mass.
Jonathan Soule,	Waterville.
*George B. Taylor,	Norridgewock.
Charles F. Webber,	Augusta.
	XIII.

1858.

Thomas F. Batchelder,	Stanton, Wis.
J. Cilley Fales,	Lebanon, Ky.
Isaac S. Hamblen,	Waterville.
Benjamin F. Lawrence,	Litchfield.
Judson W. Shaw,	Anson.
Lucius F. Shepardson,	Royalston, Mass.
Hampton D. P. Small,	Mt. Vernon.
Benjamin K. Walker,	Limington.
Jasper M. White,	St. Anthony, M. T.
	IX.

1859.

Alexander Fuller, Jr.,	Waterville.
Joseph H. Shepardson,	Royalston, Mass.
	II.

1860.

S. Hubbard Fifield,	Fayette.
John Goldthwait,	Waterville.
Henry W. Harmon,	Livermore.
John H. Jackson,	Litchfield.
R. Elvin Jones,	Jefferson.

Ransom Norton,	Livermore.
Levi M. Pierce,	West Boylston, Mass.
Stillman H. Record,	Auburn.
Edmund F. Webb,	Albion.
*George W. F. Wiggin,	Mt. Vernon.

X.

1861.

James U. Chase,	Fayette.
James B. Cochrane,	Fayette.
Granville P. Cochrane,	Monmouth.
George S. Flood,	Clinton.
Cyrus Hamlin,	Hampden.
Amos M. Jackson,	Litchfield.
Edward P. Loring,	Norridgewock.
Samuel B. Morse,	Glasgow, Ky.
Llewellyn Powers,	Pittsfield.
Bartlett Tripp,	Ripley.
Cyrus G. Warren,	Stockton.

XI.

1862.

Aretus G. Barker,	Lovell.
Wm. C. Barrows,	Litchfield.
Amasa Bigelow, Jr.,	Bloomfield.
Isaac S. Clifford,	Waterville.
Nicholas Gallagher,	Waterville.
Samuel Hamblen,	Lovell.
Edward E. Harmon,	Livermore.
N. Allen Luce,	Burnham.
J. Frank McKusick,	Denmark.
Wm. A. Merrill,	Vassalboro'.
Justin P. Moore,	Sidney.
Lewis E. Norris,	Monson.
Eli P. Noyes,	Jefferson.
John A. Philbrook,	Kendall's Mills.
Isaiah Record,	Livermore.
Adoniram J. Rich,	Cooper.
Martin B. Soule,	Waterville.
Zemro A. Smith,	Hodgdon.
Sargent S. Stearns,	Lovell.

XIX.

1863.

Ambrose Blunt,	Bristol.

NATHANIEL B. COLMAN,	Vassalboro'.
EDWIN M. COOK,	Friendship.
CHARLES M. EMERY,	Waterville.
CHARLES W. GREEN,	N. Andover, Mass.
JONATHAN J. LEAVITT,	Parsonville.
SILVANUS B. MACOMBER,	Monson.
JAMES F. NORRIS,	Monson.
MARCELLUS L. STEARNS,	Lovell.
GEORGE D. STEVENS,	Paris.
WILLIAM H. THOMPSON,	S. Parsonsfield.
	XI.

1864.

WILLIAM T. CHASE,	N. Berwick.
*CORDELLUS H. FOSS,	N. Leeds.
WILLARD W. FREEMAN,	Fairfield.
ABNER H. KEZAR,	Limerick.
HENRY C. MERRIAM,	Houlton.
BOARDMAN C. SPAULDING,	Houlton.
*EDWARD P. STEARNS,	Lovell.
MOSES W. YOUNG,	Calais.
	VIII.

1865.

*WILLIAM NIXON,	S. Paris.
	I.

1866.

EDWARD S. HUNTRESS,	Portsmouth, N. H.
HAZEN P. MCKUSICK,	Denmark.
	II.

1867.

EDWARD P. BARTLETT,	Oxford.
CORNELIUS ALBERT GOWER,	Winslow.
HENRY W. HALE,	Ellsworth.
WILLIAM K. MOODY,	Milton Plantation.
JOHN F. MOODY,	Milton Plantation.
	V.

Rochester Chapter.

Founded in 1853.

MEMBERS.

Names.	Class.	Residences.
	1853.	
*FORDYCE WILLIAMS,		Ashfield, Mass.
		I.
	1854.	
TILSON C. BARDEN,		Capt. —— Regt., N. Y. V.
SAMUEL P. FENN,		Wyandotte, Kansas.
		II.
	1855.	
WARNER H. CURTISS,		Rochester.
		I.
	1856.	
DAVID LINK,		Natural Bridge, Va.
EDWIN J. PICKETT,		Havana, N. Y.
Professor of the Natural Sciences, People's College.		
JOHN N. WHIDDEN,		Elgin, Ill.
Rev. ORLANDO WITHERSPOON,		Buffalo.
DELOS D. WOODWORTH,		Arcade.
		V.
	1857.	
Rev. M. S. B. GAGE,		Macedon.
ELI H. HURLBURT,		S. Bristol.
ROBERT A. PATTERSON,		Buffalo.
Rev. BENJAMIN W. ROGERS,		Detroit, Mich.
GEORGE TRUESDALE,		Rochester.
DAVID H. SHELDON,		St. Louis, Mo.
		VI.

1858.

Henry J. Arnold,	Somerset, N. Y.
Elon J. Douglass,	Elgin, Ill.
George G. Furgerson,	Amsterdam, N. Y.
John S. Higgins,	Flemington, N. J.
Francis B. Palmer,	Parma, N. Y.
Rev. Hugh C. Townley,	Peekskill, N. Y.
Rev. Ambrose F. Willey,	Burlington, Iowa.

VII.

1859.

*William Allen,	Shelby, N. Y.
Elmore W. Dennison,	St. Louis, Mo.
Aaron Eaker,	Sacramento, Cal.
Thomas A. Hall,	Waterford, C. W.
Daniel E. Lent,	Rochester, N. Y.
Rev. Ebenezer Packwood,	York, N. Y.
Rev. William Remington,	Weedsport, N. Y.
Rev. John M. Rice,	Elbridge, N. Y.
David H. Robinson,	Leavenworth, Ks.

Professor of Greek in Kansas University.

Daniel C. Rumsey,	Batavia, N. Y.
Rev. Winfield Scott,	Lawrence, Ks.

XI.

1860.

Francis H. Davis,	White Pigeon, Mich.
Rev. Charles E. Hewitt,	Ypsilanti, Mich.
Andrew J. Knight,	Portage, N. Y.
Rev. David H. Palmer,	Prattsburgh, N. Y.
Charles E. Richards,	Riga, N. Y.
Rev. Charles S. Sheffield,	Newfane, N. Y.
George F. Williams,	Charleston, S. C.

VII.

1861.

Rev. Abijah Baker,	Attica, N. Y.

Principal of Attica Institute.

Rev. Cyrus A. Chilcott,	Missionary to China.
Rev. Thomas Cull,	Malone, N. Y.
Rev. Francis D. Fenner,	Rochester, N. Y.
Rev. Galvin L. Hamilton,	Auburn, N. Y.
Rev. James P. Ludlow,	San Francisco, Cal.
*Charles H. Savage,	Capt. 13th N. Y. Vol.,

Killed at Bull Run, Aug. 30th, 1862.

VII.

1862.

William F. Brainbridge,	Erie, Pa.
Grove K. Gilbert,	Rochester, N. Y.
Pope C. Huntington,	Brooklyn, N. Y.
Clinton Hutchinson,	Lawrence, Kansas.
Curtis B. Parsons,	Akron, N. Y.
	V.

1863.

Rev. Albertus A. Drown,	Baraboo, Wis.
Philip P. Farnham,	Rochester Theo. Sem.
Jacob A. Hoekstra,	Rochester, N. Y.
Edwin R. Johnson,	Rochester.
Rev. Carl T. Kreyer,	American Missionary.
Silvester J. Lusk,	Walworth, N. Y.
Rev. Jerome E. Rockwood,	Sioux City, Ia.
Volney A. Sage,	Rochester, N. Y.
Donald Sinclair,	Caledonia, N. Y.
	IX.

1864.

William H. Davis,	1st Lieut. 19th U. S. Col. V.
Nehemiah N. Denton,	Canandaigua.
Charles Forbes,	Rochester, N. Y.
M. C. B. Oakley,	Philadelphia, Penn.
Lucius B. Parmele,	Marilla, N. Y.
Sereno E. Payne,	Auburn, N. Y.
Tunis D. Toan,	Spencerport, N. Y.
	VII.

1865.

William H. Allen,	Rochester, N. Y.
Wayland R. Benedict,	Rochester, N. Y.
Hamlet S. Briggs,	Rochester, N. Y.
Edwin S. Chittenden,	Albany, N. Y.
William S. Kellogg,	Pekin, Ill.
William H. Kenyon,	Mexico, N. Y.
James McWhinney, Jr.,	Waterbury, Conn.
William H. Shields,	Penn Yan.
Agustus C. Winters,	Washville, Tenn.
	IX.

1866.

Peter V. Jackson,	Irondequoit, N. Y.
Rev. Alexander B. Lamberton,	Rochester, N. Y.
	II.

1867.

Josephus W. Allen,	Barre Centre, N. Y.
LaFayette Congdon,	Springwater, N. Y.

Fernando C. Cox,	San Francisco, Cal.
Charles E. Hurlburt,	Grand Rapids, Mich.
Thomas M. Martin,	Vienna, Wis.
Charles D. Morris,	Dayton, O.
William H. Stenger,	Zanesville, O.
William H. Truesdale,	Rochester, N. Y.
Jocelyn S. Van Alstin,	Medina, N. Y.
	IX.

1868.

David Crosby,	Bath, N. Y.
William H. Davis,	Kalamazoo, Mich.
Emil Kuichling,	Rochester, N. Y.
Charles H. Palmer,	Rochester, N. Y.
Reuben Stiles,	Climax, Mich.
	V.

1869.

Samuel E. Baldwin,	Albion, N. Y.
Forrest A. Marsh,	Austin, Minn.
Joseph M. McMaster,	Rochester, N. Y.
William E. Wayte,	Rochester, N. Y.
Theodore B. Williams,	Avoca, N. Y.
Linus Woolverston,	Grenisly, C. W.
	VI.

1870.

Will H. Sloan,	Leavenworth, Ks.
	I.

Middlebury Chapter.

Founded in 1856.

MEMBERS.

Names.	*Class.*	*Residences.*
	1857.	
Rev. WARREN W. WINCHESTER,		Middlebury, Vt.
Hon. JOHN W. PHELPS,		Brattleboro, Vt.
Rev. ALANSON S. BARTON,		Saxton's River, Vt.
THOMAS HERBERT DAVIS,		Henrico Co., Va.
Rev. JEREMIAH N. DIAMENT,		Pierpoint, N. Y.
LOYAL DORUS ELDRIDGE,		Middlebury, Vt.
HENRY SMITH FOOTE,		Middlebury, Vt.
NEHEMIAH WHITE,		Canton, N. Y.
	Professor in Canton College.	
Rev. AZEL W. WILD,		Greensboro, Vt.
		IX.
	1858.	
*Rev. CHARLES F. ABBOTT,		Bristol, N. Y.
GEORGE FISHER,		Alton, Ill.
Rev. CALVIN H. FLOWER,		Parishville, N. Y.
*DANIEL M. HOWARD,		Benson, Vt.
Rev. GEORGE A. ROCKWOOD,		Carthage, N. Y.
JULIUS WILCOX,		Brooklyn, N. Y.
		VI.
	1859.	
Rev. JOHN G. BAILEY,		Hyde Park, Vt.
SILAS LEROY BLAKE,		Pepperell, Mass.
*Capt. M. P. S. CADWELL,		New Haven, Vt.
GEORGE ERASTUS LANE,		Williamston, Vt.

Rev. Seth W. Segur,	Royalton, Ohio.
Rev. Milton L. Severance,	Boscawen, N. H.
Lyman S. Watts,	Peacham, Vt.
	VII.

1860.

Bovelte Bardeaux Bishop,	Lewis, N. Y.
Rev. Henry P. Higley,	Beloit, Wis.
Rev. Giles F. Montgomery,	Aintab, Turkey.
Elijah B. Sherman,	Chicago, Ill.
Charles Gutzlaff Steele,	Middlebury, Vt.
Rev. John Bacon Steele,	Castile, N. Y.
Henry H. Vail,	Cincinnati, Ohio.
Rev. Edward Payson Wild,	Craftsbury, Vt.
Rev. John Kilbourn Williams,	Bradford, Vt.
	IX.

1861.

Joseph G. Colt,	Brookfield, Vt.
*James T. Gove,	Lincoln, Vt.
*George E. Joslin,	Vergennes, Vt.
Rev. Moses M. Martin,	Middletown, Vt.
Rev. S. B. Partridge,	Wales, Mass.
Lyman W. Peet,	Hoboken, N. H.
Rev. James E. Pierce,	Auburn, N. Y.
Adjunct Professor of Hebrew in Auburn Theo. Sem.	
Lines E. Sherman,	Ludlow, Vt.
	VIII.

1862.

Enos L. Knapp,	Middlebury, Vt.
Rev. William Albert Robinson,	Boston, Vt.
*Arthur T. Wilder,	Dixmont, Me.
	III.

1863.

*Lieut. Albert A. Crane,	Bridport, Vt.
George Graham,	La Crosse, Wis.
Daniel Webster Holmes,	Hubbardton, Vt.
W. H. Proctor,	Fairhaven, Vt.
Rev. Frank Hiram Seeley,	Richville Springs, N. Y.
	V.

1864.

Rev. George H. Bailey,	Brattleboro, Vt.
*Henry W. Bennett,	Middlebury, Vt.
Francis M. Edgerton,	New York City.
Calvin Day Noble,	Cairo, Ill.
Charles Edward Prentiss,	Washington, D. C.
	V.

1865.

Ezekiel Webster Dimond,	Concord, N. H.

*Henry Jonas Flint,	Dalton, Mass.
Evarts B. Kent,	Auburn Theo. Sem.
William Henry Rand,	Keene, N. H.
Henry Hattric Shaw,	Chester, Vt.
	V.

1866.

Willard Deming Brown,	Auburn Theo. Sem.
John Wesley Lovett,	Middlebury, Vt.
Nathan Round Nichols,	Castleton, Vt.
Merritt Bates Page,	Oregon, Wis.
Leroy M. Pierce,	Auburn Theo. Sem.
Eugene John Ranston,	Auburn Theo. Sem.
	VI.

1867.

Cyrus Clark Boynton,	Springfield, Vt.
L. Vernon Ferris,	Lawrenceville, N. Y.
	II.

1868.

Charles Nash Bell,	Weybridge, Vt.
Alfred Erastus Higley,	Castleton, Vt.
Edwin Hall Higley,	Castleton, Vt.
Charles Henry Rowley,	Middlebury, Vt.
	IV.

1869.

Henry Sylvester Baker,	Danby, Vt.
Martin E. Cady,	Middlebury, Vt.
Anthony Cass,	Middlebury, Vt.
Rufus Cushman Flagg,	Castleton, Vt.
	IV.

1870.

Martin Egbert Severance,	Middlebury, Vt.
Eugene Frank Wright,	Shorsham, Vt.
	II.

Bowdoin Chapter.

Founded in 1858.

MEMBERS.

Names.	*Class.*	*Residences.*
	1858.	
William Allen Abbott,		Norridgewock.
Lysander Hill,		Cushing.
George Robinson McIntyre,		Newton Theo. Sem.
Edwin Reed,		Bangor Theo. Sem.
Isaiah Perley Smith,		Bridgton.
Ellis Spear,		Warren.
		VI.
	1860.	
Edwin A. Harlow,		East Hebron.
Winthrop Norton,		Norridgewock.
Levi R. Leavitt,		Meredith, N. H.
Charles F. Penny,		New Gloucester.
James L. Phillips,		Iowa City, Ia.
		V.
	1861.	
John E. Butler,		Meredith, N. H.
Nelson P. Cram,		Bridgton.
Albert D. F. Palmer,		North Anson.
Gustavus S. Palmer,		North Anson.
Reuben A. Rideout,		Garland.
Henry S. B. Smith,		Bridgton.
Sylvanus D. Waterman,		Litchfield.
Marcus Wight, Jr.,		Brunswick.
		VIII.
	1862.	
Samuel W. Pearson,		Alna.
		I.

Rutgers Chapter.

Founded in 1858.

MEMBERS.

Names.	*Class.*	*Residences.*
	1859.	
W. H. Bartles,		Flemington, N. J.
Rev. J. R. Brock,		Spring Valley, N. Y.
Rev. Alonzo P. Peek,		Owasco, N. Y.
Rev. J. Kelly Rhinehart,		Roxbury, N. Y.
Rev. Samuel J. Rogers,		Geneva, N. Y.
Rev. A. J. Sebring,		Mellenville, N. Y.
J. Howard Van Doren,		Missionary at Amoy, China.
Rev. H. M. Voorhees,		Albany, N. Y.
		VIII.
	1860.	
Rev. John W. Beardslee,		Constantine, Mich.
Josiah J. Brown,		Union Theo. Sem. N. Y.
Rev. Richard Dewitt,		Tuthill, N. Y.
Rev. Andrew J. Hagaman,		Hagaman's Mills, N. Y.
Rev. Wm. Jones Skillman,		Tecumseh, Mich.
Abraham Suydam,		Trenton, N. J.
Rev. Egbert Winter,		Pella, Iowa.
		VII.
	1861.	
G. De Witt Bodine,		Richboro, Penn.
*John W. Borst,		Middleburgh, N. Y.
James Wyckoff,		Queens, N. Y.
		III.

1862.

Robert B. Kinsell,	Patterson, N. J.
Charles H. Riggs,	Warwick, N. Y.
Rev. John V. N. Schenk,	Auburn, N. Y.
Rev. Elbert N. Sebring,	Hudson, N. Y.
Rev. N. Hixon Van Arsdale,	Pluckamin, N. J.
Jacob H. Van Ness,	Pompton Plains, N. J.
Rev. William H. Vroom,	Hoboken, N. J.
	VII.

1863.

Rev. George A. Mills,	Copakee, N. Y.
Rev. Charles H. Pool,	Pluckamin, N. J.
Rev. George W. Swain,	Middlebush, N. J.
	III.

1864.

Rev. James H. Bertholf,	Philadelphia, Pa.
Benjamin F. Decker,	Goshen, N. Y.
Jared Hasbrouck,	Alligerville, N. Y.
Rev. Thomas W. Jones,	East Chatham, N. Y.
William H. Kling,	Brooklyn, L. I.
T. L. Stringer,	Britan, N. J.
	VII.

1865.

Henry J. Brown, Jr.,	Detroit, Mich.
John A. Davis,	Theo.Sem.NewBrunswick.
Thomas L. Gulick,	Honolulu, Sand. Is.
Adrian Westveer,	Theo.Sem.NewBrunswick.
	IV.

1866.

A. Augustus Bookstaver,	Theo. Sem. Princeton.
*Charles P. Demorest,	Warwick, N. Y.
Peter V. Van Buskirk,	Theo.Sem.NewBrunswick.
	III.

1867.

Samuel R. Demarest,	Closter, N. J.
Benjamin C. Nevius,	Stuyvesant, N. Y.
	II.

1868.

Daniel Talmage, Jr.,	Bound Brook, N. J.
	I.

1869.

William E. Griffis,	Philadelphia, Penn.
John Hart,	Richboro, Penn.
Charles Luman Knapp,	Lowville, N. Y.

George Warne Labaw,	Harlingen, N. J.
Edward Lodewick,	East Greenbush, N. Y.
George W. Robinson,	Tottenville, N. Y.

VI.

1870.

Luther Barton,	Dayton, N. J.
John G. Cortelyou,	Harlingen, N. J.
Henry N. Marsh,	New Brunswick, N. J.
John F. McLaury,	Delhi, N. Y.
Nicholas Pearse,	Lishas Kill, N. Y.
R. A. Pearse,	Lishas Kill, N. Y.
Jacob W. Schenk,	New Brunswick, N. J.

VII.

Jefferson Chapter.

Founded in 1859.

MEMBERS.

Names.	*Class.*	*Residences.*
Rev. Edsall Ferris, Professor of English Literature.		Pennsylvania College,
	1860.	
Rev. Albert Dilworth,		Enon Valley, Pa.
Rev. Robert Todd McMahon,		Warsaw, Ill.
*James W. Melvin,		New Castle, Pa.
John Steele Paxton,		Grandview, Ill.
		IV.
	1861.	
Rev. William C. Kuhn,		Walcott, Ia.
John W. Laughlin,		Washington, O.
Rev. Joseph A. Leyenberger,		Nashville, O.
Rev. David M. McClellan,		West Hebron, N. Y.
		IV.
	1862.	
Rev. Albert Johnson Caldwell,		Soughioghany, Pa.
Rev. Stephen A. Califf,		East Smithfield, Pa.
Rev. Stephen P. Gates,		Rome, Pa.
James P. McVickar,		White Hall, Pa.
James G. Sloan,		Washington, D. C.
John Sumney,		Dunningsville, Pa.
		VI.
	1863.	
Hugh W. Boyd,		Clockeyville, Pa.
John J. Jordan,		Good Intent, Pa.
Rev. Hugh Y. Leiper,		Hookstown, Pa.

*Samuel T. Robinson,	Raymond, Miss.
Thomas H. Stewart,	Murraysville, Pa.
Robert L. Stewart,	Canonsburg, Pa.
*Hugh Weir,	Strabane, Pa.
	VII.

1864.

George F. Baker,	Steeleville, Pa.
James Potter Barron,	Buchanan, W. Va.
James Black,	Canonsburg, Pa.
Rev. Augustine Breese,	Ottawa, Ill.
Rev. Robert M. Brown,	Allegheny City, Pa.
Rev. Eben Caldwell,	Soughioghany, Pa.
Rev. William H. Gill,	Allegheny City, Pa.
Rev. Charles Knepper,	Steinsville, Pa.
Robert E. Sharp,	Newville, Pa.
George M. Templeton,	Canonsburg, Pa.
Rev. Alex. Scroggs Thompson,	Newville, Pa.
Dickson Reynolds Waggoner,	Pulaski, Pa.
	XII.

1865.

Ahaz N. Alcott,	Gowanda, N. Y.
Professor of Elocution.	
Patterson T. Caldwell,	Youngstown, O.
Charles F. W. Cranemeyer,	Allegheny City, Pa.
James Grier, Jr.,	Noblestown, Pa.
Thomas Hindman,	Dayton, Pa.
S. Hunter McKown,	Gerrardstown, Va.
Robert P. Shaw,	Bellefontain, O.
	VII.

1866.

John Anderson,	Pittsburgh, Pa.
Samuel M. Davis,	Ebenezer, Pa.
William J. Hamilton,	Lexington, Pa.
R. C. McPherson,	Alleghany City, Pa.
William J. Myers,	Steubenville, O.
J. Douglas Shafer,	Bakerstown, Pa.
Charles H. Smith,	Franklin, Ind.
Robert L. Stewart,	Murraysville, Pa.
Johnson E. Walter,	West Newton, Pa.
John U. Wilson,	Salem, O.
	X.

1867.

James L. Black,	Cannonsburgh, Pa.
Bankhead Boyd,	Clokeyville, Pa.

John A. Campbell,	New Cumberland, W. Va.
D. R. McKnight, Jr.,	Mt. Lebanon, Pa.
E. E. Rivpel,	Toledo, O.
James Herron Scott,	Bural Hill, Pa.
	VI.

1868.

J. Edgar Stevenson Bell,	Finleyville, Va.
Edward Gray Comingo,	Steubenville, O.
Neville B. C. Comingo,	Steubenville, O.
David B. Fleming,	Indianapolis, Pa.
John M. French,	Canonsburgh, Pa.
Enoch South Gaus,	New Geneva, Pa.
John S. Glendenning,	Canonsburgh, Pa.
Joseph D. Wilson,	North Bend, Wis.
	VIII.

1869.

Silas Cooke,	Cross Creek, Pa.
Andrew Steele Miller,	Canonsburgh, Pa.
J. Kirk Pierce,	Marion, Ia.
Elmer Poulson,	Holmesville, O.
	IV.

New York Chapter.

Founded in 1865.

MEMBERS.

Names.	*Class.*	*Residences.*
Rev. Isaac Ferris,		New York City,
Chancellor of New York University.		
Rev. Henry M. Baird,		New York City.
Professor of Greek, New York University.		
	1865.	
Thomas Burnet,		New York City.
		I.
	1866.	
Chalmers D. Chapman,		Irvington, N. J.
Samuel B. Duryea,		Brooklyn, L. I.
S. Gedney Keyser,		New York City.
Isaac Ferris Ludlam,		New York City.
John Ogle, Jr.,		Stapleton, L. I.
Henry Spellinger, Jr.,		New Brighton, L. I.
		VI.
	1867.	
James F. Rhodes,		Cleveland, Ohio.
F. A. Wood,		Brooklyn, L. I.
		II.
	1868.	
E. S. T. Kennedy,		New York City.
John Love, Jr.,		New York City.
Wm. Leslie Ludlam,		New York City.
John B. Talmage,		Green Point, L. I.
James C. Thompson,		New York City.
		V.

1869.

R. W. Haskins,	New York City.
Charles Edward Hore,	Brooklyn, L. I.
J. W. Root,	New York City.
N. B. Sizer,	Brooklyn, L. I.

IV.

1870.

John Reid,	New York City.
John C. Vandwenter,	Jersey City, N. J.

II.

Western Reserve Chapter.

Founded in 1865.

MEMBERS.

Names.	*Class.*	*Residences.*
	1866.	
George F. Fitch,		Fremont, O.
Heber A. Ketchum,		Norwalk, O.
John N. Wilson,		Salem, O.
		III.
	1867.	
William A. Comstock,		Cuyahoga Falls, O.
John H. Jones,		Youngstown, O.
		II.
	1868.	
Hermon Bronson,		Peninsular, O.
Fred. B. Buss,		Hudson, O.
George Lee,		Hudson, O.
		III.
	1869.	
Herbert W. Bill,		Cuyahoga Falls, O.
Addison M. Chapin,		Spartansburgh, Pa.
Avery Gallup,		Cleveland, O.
Sinclair J. Hatfield,		Apple Creek, O.
J. Ernest Julian,		Cleveland, O.
George E. King,		Ravenna, O.
Howard R. Parmalee,		Twinsburgh, O.
Josiah Strong,		Hudson, O.
		VIII.
	1870.	
Marcus Coyad,		Cleveland, O.
John Mc. R. Robinson,		Calhoun, Ill.
F. Dwight Seward,		Maukato, Minn.
William F. Sliney,		Cleveland, O.
		IV.

Madison Chapter.

Founded in 1866.

MEMBERS.

Names.	Class.	Residences.
	1866.	
CHARLES T. EATON,		Hamilton, N. Y.
GEORGE L. C. HANNA,		New York City.
ELISHA P. HICKOK,		Guilford, Mo.
Professor of Mathematics and Languages, Burlington Academy, Ia.		
WILLIAM S. MITCHELL,		Montrose, Pa.
CLARK B. OAKLEY,		Bound Brook, N. Y.
D. D. OWEN,		Central Square, N. Y.
HENRY H. PEABODY,		Wenham, Mass.
WILLIAM G. WALKER,		Jonnsons Creek, N. Y.
		VIII.
	1867.	
CHARLES E. BECKER,		Micklenburgh, N. Y.
JAMES M. TAYLOR,		Holmdel, N. Y.
		II.
	1868.	
JOSEPH H. SHOARDS,		New York City.
		I.
	1869.	
EDWARD K. CHANDLER,		McMinnville, Oregon.
JAMES W. FORD,		Preston Hollow, N. J.
SILAS W. HATCH,		Madrid, N. Y.
W. WAYLAND PATTENGILL,		West Winfield, N. Y.
JABEZ SNASHALL,		Sherman, N. Y.
NELSON SUTTON,		Webster, N. Y.

George A. Thomas,	Norwich, N. Y.
George O. Whitney,	Brooklyn, N. Y.
	VIII.

1870

Francis M. Beebee,	Erieville, N. Y.
William T. C. Hanna,	New York City.
Henry C. Leach,	Harpersville, N. Y.
John F. Murphy,	Sandisfield, Mass.
Theodore Truvé,	Gottenburgh, Sweedèn.
	V.

Washington Chapter.

Founded in 1866.

MEMBERS.

Names.	*Class.*	*Residences.*
	1868.	
Casius C. Cozad,		Van Buren, Pa.
John A. McKean,		Washington, Pa.
John M. Oliver,		Van Buren, Pa.
Walter J. Scott,		Smithfield, O.
David M. Welday,		Wintersville, O.
William H. Welday,		Wintersville, O.
		VI.
	1869.	
William H. Hartzell,		Washington, Pa.
George O. Jones,		Washington, Pa.
		II.
	1870.	
James H. Clark,		Youngstown, O.
Griffith H. Humphrey,		Ixonia Center, Wis.
Albert S. Leonard,		Parkersburgh, W. Va.
Chester P. Murray,		West Alexander, Ha.
William T. McConnell,		West Middletown, Pa.
Georfe F. Sonner,		Hillsboro, O.

INDEX.

Apthorp, Rufus	1857	*Williams.*
Arnold, Henry J.	1856	*Rochester.*
Aspinwall, Judson	1854	*Williams.*
Atkins, Nelson F.	1845	*Williams.*
Atwood, A. Watson	1863	*Union.*
Austin, James M.	1838	*Union.*
Austin, H. A.	1845	*Union.*
Austin, S. J.	1845	*Union.*
Austin, Charles B.	1868	*Hamilton.*
Avery, Nelson N.	1855	*Hamilton.*
Avery, Truman G.	1856	*Hamilton.*
Avery, James B.	1867	*Hamilton.*
Bacheldor, John M.	1849	*Williams.*
Bacon, Thomas S.	1842	*Williams.*
Bacon, Henry M.	1845	*Williams.*
Bacon, Charles F.	1847	*Williams.*
Bailey, John G.	1859	*Middlebury.*
Bailey, Edward L.	1851	*Union.*
Bailey, George H.	1864	*Middlebury.*
Bainbridge, William F.	1858	*Rochester.*
Baird, Henry M.	——	*New York.*
Baker, James S.	1857	*Hamilton.*
Baker, Abijah	1855	*Rochester.*
Baker, Henry S.	——	
Baker, Alvin	1859	*Hamilton.*
Baker, George F.	1864	*Jefferson.*
Baldwin, Algernon S.	1845	*Williams.*
Baldwin, Henry W.	1836	*Williams.*
Baldwin, William O.	1851	*Amherst.*
Baldwin, Samuel E.	1869	*Rochester.*
Ball, Charles B.	1846	*Williams.*
Ballard, Addison	1842	*Williams.*
Bangs, Egbert L.	1851	*Hamilton.*
Bannard, John	1845	*Union.*
Banta, Arie	1845	*Union.*
Barden, Tilson C.	1853	*Rochester.*
Barker, Aretus G.	1862	*Waterville.*
Barker, Henry J.	1844	*Williams.*
Barnes, Albert	1820	*Hamilton.*
Barnes, Henry E.	1860	*Amherst.*
Barkley, Samuel	1849	*Union.*
Barron, James Potter	1864	*Jefferson.*
Barrows, William C.	1862	*Waterville.*
Bartles, W. H.	1859	*Rutgers.*
Bartlett, Edward P.	1867	*Waterville.*
Bartlett, George	1838	*Union.*
Bartlett, P. Mason	1850	*Williams.*
Bartlett, Lyman	1856	*Amherst.*
Barton, Alanson S.	1857	*Middlebury.*
Barton, Luther	1870	*Rutgers.*

Bigelow, Osborn P.	1853	*Waterville.*
Bill, Herbert W.	1869	*Western Reserve.*
Billings, Sanford W.	1859	*Amherst.*
Bird, John M.	1838	*Union.*
Bishop, Bovett	1860	*Middlebury.*
Bishop, John C.	1848	*Union.*
Bissell, Benjamin	1858	*Williams.*
Bissell, Charles H.	1858	*Williams.*
Bixby, Joseph P.	1858	*Williams.*
Black, James	1864	*Jefferson.*
Blackmer, Andrew C.	1853	*Williams.*
Blair, Austin	1838	*Union.*
Blain, David	1859	*Hamilton.*
Blake, H. B.	1841	*Williams.*
Blake, Silas L.	1859	*Middlebury.*
Blake, J. Albert	1862	*Williams.*
Blakely, A. J.	1858	*Union.*
Blakely, Collins	1858	*Union.*
Blakely, S. E.	1858	*Union.*
Blanchard, William D.	1847	*Williams.*
Blanchard, Nathaniel B.	1853	*Amherst.*
Bliss, Thomas E.	1846	*Union.*
Bliss, Daniel	1852	*Amherst.*
Bliss, LeRoy	1850	*Hamilton.*
Bliss, Daniel	1858	*Amherst.*
Bliss, Porter C.	1861	*Hamilton.*
Blodgett, Henry F.	1857	*Amherst.*
Bloomer, Joseph	1856	*Amherst.*
Blunt, Ambrose	1863	*Waterville.*
Bodine, J. De Witt	1861	*Rutgers.*
Bodman, Albert H.	1848	*Williams.*
Bogardus, Eri	1846	*Williams.*
Boies, Reuben B.	1843	*Williams.*
Boies, Fisher A.	1849	*Williams.*
Bookstaver, A. Augustus	1866	*Rutgers.*
Boomer, Norton W.	1859	*Hamilton.*
Borst, John W.	1861	*Rutgers.*
Bosworth, Byron	1850	*Hamilton.*
Bosworth, Daniel	1863	*Union.*
Bottsford, Alfred P.	1845	*Union.*
Bottsford, Eli C.	1846	*Union.*
Bowman, Harlow	1855	*Union.*
Boyd, Bankhead	1867	*Jefferson.*
Boyd, Hugh W.	1863	*Jefferson.*
Boynton, Cyrus	1867	*Middlebury.*
Boynton, Reuben L.	1846	*Union.*
Boynton, Henry B.	1852	*Hamilton.*
Boynton, Francis H.	1861	*Amherst.*
Bradbury, William F.	1856	*Amherst.*
Bradbury, Edward E.	1856	*Amherst.*

Burnet, Thomas	1865	*New York.*
Burnett, Theodore W.	1853	*Hamilton.*
Burr, Henry B.	1847	*Union.*
Burrall, George W.	1838	*Williams.*
Burt, James M.	1840	*Williams.*
Burt, Evelyn A.	1847	*Williams.*
Burt, J. B.	1858	*Union.*
Bush, Stephen	1845	*Williams.*
Buss, Fred B.	1868	*Western Reserve.*
Butler, John E.	1861	*Bowdoin.*
Butts, J. T.	1858	*Union.*
Buttz, Henry A.	1855	*Union.*
Cadwell, M. P. S.	1859	*Middlebury.*
Cady, Martin E.	1869	*Middlebury.*
Cady, George M.	1840	*Williams.*
Calderwood, William N.	1845	*Union.*
Caldwell, Eben	1864	*Jefferson.*
Caldwell, Patterson I.	1865	*Jefferson.*
Caldwell Albert J.	1862	*Jefferson.*
Caldwell, John C.	1855	*Amherst.*
Califf, Stephen A.	1862	*Jefferson.*
Calkins, James F.	1838	*Union.*
Camp, Samuel C.	1850	*Hamilton.*
Camp, Samuel	1858	*Hamilton.*
Camp, Cyrus C.	1858	*Hamilton.*
Cameron, Duncan E.	1845	*Union.*
Cameron, John J.	1851	*Union.*
Campbell, D.	1839	*Union.*
Campbell, John A.	1867	*Jefferson.*
Campbell, John	1849	*Hamilton.*
Canfield, Philo	1836	*Williams.*
Cannon, Horace	1860	*Amherst.*
Carmichael, John	1845	*Union.*
Carleton, Marcus M.	1851	*Amherst.*
Carr, William O.	1857	*Amherst.*
Carrington, George M.	1861	*Williams.*
Carter Charles M.	1862	*Union.*
Carter, Lucian E.	1856	*Union.*
Carter, John H.	1858	*Union.*
Cary, John W.	1838	*Union.*
Case, Ira	1848	*Amherst.*
Cass, Anthony	1869	*Middlebury.*
Cavert, M. P.	1839	*Union.*
Chandler, Howard K.	1869	*Madison.*
Chapin, Joseph Y.	1866	*Hamilton.*
Chapin, Addison M.	1869	*Western Reserve.*
Chapman, Chalmers D.	1866	*New York.*
Chase, William I.	1864	*Waterville.*
Chase, Hiram	1843	*Williams.*
Chase, F. A.	1854	*Union.*

Chase, James U.	1861	*Waterville.*
Chadbourne, J. S.	1840	*Union.*
Chadsey, Demetrius M.	1839	*Union.*
Chamberlain, J. F.	1838	*Union.*
Chamberlain, Albert	1849	*Williams.*
Chamberlain, Luman B.	1851	*Union.*
Champlin, Edward W.	1838	*Union.*
Chapin, William W.	1860	*Williams.*
Chapman, Orlow W.	1851	*Union.*
Chapman, Charles H.	1855	*Union.*
Chichester, Darwin	1838	*Union.*
Chilcott, Cyrus A.	1861	*Rochester.*
Child, William C.	1838	*Union.*
Childes, Albert L.	1861	*Hamilton.*
Chipman, Walter	1839	*Union.*
Chittenden, Edwin S.	1865	*Rochester.*
Clapp, Luther	1841	*Williams.*
Clapp, Jacob C.	1857	*Amherst.*
Clapp, Andrew J.	1858	*Amherst.*
Clark, L. Brainard	1870	*Hamilton.*
Clark, Solomon	1837	*Williams.*
Clark, T. Jarvis	1836	*Williams.*
Clark, George W.	1853	*Amherst.*
Clark, George W.	1838	*Union.*
Clark, James H.	1870	*Washington.*
Clark, George	1843	*Williams.*
Clark, Theodore	1839	*Williams.*
Clark, Charles K.	1843	*Williams.*
Clark, Anson,	1845	*Williams.*
Clark, Edgar W.	1848	*Williams.*
Clark, Joseph M.	1852	*Amherst.*
Clark, Rowan	1852	*Williams.*
Clark, James A.	1853	*Williams.*
Clark, Walter H.	1854	*Williams.*
Clark, Joseph L.	1852	*Union.*
Clark, Ethan	1853	*Union.*
Clark, Asahel L.	1857	*Amherst.*
Clark, Royal W.	1858	*Amherst.*
Clark, Edward	1837	*Williams.*
Clark, Elias	1836	*Williams.*
Clark, William J.	1861	*Amherst.*
Clarke, George C.	1858	*Amherst.*
Clarke, Edward S.	1837	*Williams.*
Clason, S. Webb	1864	*Rutgers.*
Cleveland, Giles B.	1850	*Hamilton.*
Cleveland, Guy K.	1850	*Hamilton.*
Clegg, John C.	1846	*Williams.*
Clifford, Isaac S.	1862	*Waterville.*
Clisby, George,	1836	*Williams.*
Close, M. H.	1859	*Union.*

Coan, George M.	1849	*Williams.*
Coan, George W.	1846	*Williams.*
Cochrane, Granville P.	1861	*Waterville.*
Cochrane, James B.	1861	*Waterville.*
Cole, William H.	1839	*Union.*
Colman, Nathaniel B.	1863	*Waterville.*
Collins, Barnabas	1840	*Williams.*
Collins, James	1858	*Amherst.*
Colt, Joseph G.	1861	*Middlebury.*
Comengo, Edward C.	1868	*Jefferson.*
Comfort, Lawrence L.	1846	*Union.*
Comingo, William B. C.	1868	*Western Reserve.*
Comstock, William A.	1867	*Western Reserve.*
Condit, Uzal W.	1847	*Williams.*
Conforth, Linton C.	1855	*Waterville.*
Conforth, Columbus	1856	*Waterville.*
Congdon, La Fayette	1866	*Rochester.*
Conklin, Timothy	1838	*Union.*
Connit, George W.	1848	*Williams.*
Constantine, George	1859	*Amherst.*
Converse, James	1850	*Hamilton.*
Converse, John R.	1862	*Middlebury.*
Cook, Edwin M.	1863	*Waterville.*
Cook, Henry P.	1863	*Hamilton.*
Cook, James H.	1839	*Union.*
Cooke, Silas	1869	*Western Reserve.*
Cooke, Theodore	1843	*Williams.*
Coon, Henry P.	1844	*Williams.*
Coolidge, Amos H.	1853	*Amherst.*
Cooley, Edwin	1854	*Amherst.*
Cooley, O. Wellington	1841	*Williams.*
Copeland, Jonathan	1839	*Union.*
Cory, John E.	1850	*Amherst.*
Corthell, William J.	1857	*Waterville.*
Cortelyou, John G.	1870	*Rutgers.*
Cornwall, Augustus	1840	*Williams.*
Cornwell, Amos R.	1853	*Union.*
Corwin, Eli	1848	*Williams.*
Cowles, Augustus W.	1838	*Union.*
Cowles, George R.	1845	*Williams.*
Cowper, James S.	1845	*Union.*
Cozard, Cassius C.	1868	*Washington.*
Cozard, Marcus	1870	*Western Reserve.*
Cox, Fernando C.	1867	*Rochester.*
Craig, Adam	1839	*Union.*
Cram, Nelson P.	1861	*Bowdoin.*
Crandall, Uberto	1839	*Union.*
Crane, Albert A.	1863	*Middlebury.*
Crane, David F.	1855	*Waterville.*
Crane, A. Robinson	1856	*Waterville.*

Demond, Charles	1844	*Williams.*
Demorest, Samuel N.	1868	*Rutgers.*
Demorest, Chas. P.	1866	*Rutgers.*
Denio, Cole Herman	1835	*Williams.*
Denison, Elmore W.	1858	*Rochester.*
Denniston, Jr., Robert	1855	*Union.*
Denton, Nehemiah N.	1864	*Rochester.*
Denton, Theodore J.	1845	*Williams.*
Devereaux, Alvin	1841	*Williams.*
Dewell, Jacob B.	1848	*Williams.*
Dewing, Thomas S.	1847	*Williams.*
De Witt, Abner	1851	*Williams.*
De Witt, Richard	1860	*Rutgers.*
Deyoe, Ephraim	1838	*Union.*
Diament, Jeremiah N.	1857	*Middlebury.*
Dibble, Seymour H.	1862	*Hamilton.*
Dibble, Cassius M.	1868	*Hamilton.*
Dickinson, Edward A.	1839	*Williams.*
Dickson, Alexander	1845	*Union.*
Dill, William H.	1862	*Rutgers.*
Dilley, Alexander	1843	*Williams.*
Dillingham, John H.	1857	*Hamilton.*
Dilworth, Albert	1860	*Jefferson.*
Dimock, Edwin	1854	*Amherst.*
Dimon, Oliver	1840	*Williams.*
Dimon, Nathan	1870	*Madison.*
Dimond, Ezekiel	1865	*Middlebury.*
Dobbin, James S.	1845	*Union.*
Dodd, Cyrus M.	1849	*Williams.*
Dodge, Edward C.	1846	*Union.*
Doe, Franklin B.	1851	*Amherst.*
Donaldson, John	1838	*Union.*
Donaldson, John C.	1852	*Hamilton.*
Donnan, William G.	1853	*Union.*
Donnelly, J. Bogardus	1843	*Williams.*
Douglass, Jr., Eben	1851	*Amherst.*
Douglass, Francis A.	1851	*Amherst.*
Douglass, Elon C.	1855	*Rochester.*
Dow, James	1839	*Union.*
Dow, George W.	1852	*Waterville.*
Downing, William Lee	1869	*Hamilton.*
Drake, J. Murray	1857	*Waterville.*
Drown, Albertus A.	1863	*Rochester.*
Dubois, John	1838	*Union.*
Dunbar, James	1839	*Union.*
Dunning, Charles S.	1848	*Williams.*
Dunton, Frederick B.	1856	*Waterville.*
Duryea, Samuel B.	1866	*New York.*
Eacker, William E.	1839	*Union.*
Eaker, Aaron	1855	*Rochester.*

Fisher, S. W.	1841	*Williams.*
Fisher, James P.	1838	*Union.*
Fitch, Appleton H.	1855	*Amherst.*
Fitch, G. W.	1858	*Union.*
Fitch, George W.	1862	*Union.*
Fitch, George F.	1866	*Western Reserve.*
Flagg, Rufus C.	1869	*Middleburg.*
Flagg, William D.	1853	*Amherst.*
Fleming, David B.	1868	*Jefferson.*
Fletcher, Augustus A.	1857	*Waterville.*
Fling, W. Earl	1843	*Williams.*
Flint, Ephraim	1851	*Williams.*
Flint, Franklin C.	1861	*Amherst.*
Flint, Frederick W.	1855	*Union.*
Flint, Henry J.	1865	*Middlebury.*
Flower, Calvin H.	1858	*Middlebury.*
Flood, George S.	1861	*Waterville.*
Fobes, William A.	1848	*Amherst.*
Folsom, G. P.	1847	*Williams.*
Fonda, Anthony C.	1838	*Union.*
Foord, Henry	1865	*Hamilton.*
Foote, Henry S.	1857	*Middlebury.*
Forbes, Charles	1864	*Rochester.*
Forbes Samuel B.	1854	*Williams.*
Ford, Jonathan	1839	*Williams.*
Ford, Henry A.	1842	*Williams.*
Ford, J. Edwards	1844	*Williams.*
Ford, James W.	1869	*Madison.*
Ford, Chandler T.	1848	*Williams.*
Ford, Edward J.	1849	*Williams.*
Ford, F. F.	1852	*Williams.*
Ford, Francis F.	1851	*Hamilton.*
Ford, Joseph C.	1851	*Hamilton.*
Ford, Henry T.	1858	*Williams.*
Ford, Henry A.	1862	*Amherst.*
Foskett, Horace B.	1854	*Williams.*
Foss, Cordellus R.	1864	*Waterville.*
Foster, S. Hildreth	1842	*Williams.*
Foster, Joseph C.	1849	*Williams.*
Fountain, C. H.	1843	*Williams.*
Fowler, Spencer J.	1849	*Union.*
Fradenburgh, Stephen	1846	*Union.*
Frazer, Thomas	1840	*Union.*
Freeman, H. Woodward	1845	*Union.*
Freeman, Willard W.	1864	*Waterville.*
Freeman, William F.	1854	*Union.*
French, John W.	1868	*Jefferson.*
Frost, D. D.	1840	*Williams.*
Fry, Jacob	1849	*Union.*
Fuller, Robert	1838	*Union.*

Grant, Gabriel	1846	*Williams.*
Gray, John G.	1851	*Union.*
Gray, Robert	1846	*Union.*
Gray, William C.	1856	*Hamilton.*
Green, Charles W.	1863	*Waterville.*
Green, Daniel C.	1843	*Williams.*
Green, Emery C.	1838	*Union.*
Green, James	1844	*Williams.*
Greenfield, DeLinton W.	1868	*Hamilton.*
Greves, J. Sandford	1861	*Hamilton.*
Griebel, John D.	1863	*Rochester.*
Grier, Jr. James	1865	*Jefferson.*
Griffiths, William E.	1869	*Rutgers.*
Griggs, Charles E.	1856	*Amherst.*
Griswold, Alpha D.	1855	*Williams.*
Griswold, John V.	1865	*Union.*
Griswold, Wolcott M.	1852	*Union.*
Guernsey, George M.	1856	*Amherst.*
Guffin, Cyrus	1844	*Williams.*
Gulick, Thomas L.	1865	*Rutgers.*
Gunn, Walter	1839	*Union.*
Guthrie, James	1857	*Williams.*
Hackley, Simeon	1853	*Hamilton.*
Hadden, Alexander	1854	*Union.*
Hageman, Andrew J.	1860	*Rutgers.*
Hale, Henry W.	1867	*Waterville.*
Hale, James R.	1853	*Amherst.*
Hall, Thomas A.	1838.	*Williams.*
Hall, David B.	1838	*Union.*
Hall, Ephraim C.	1840	*Union.*
Hall, C. M.	1845	*Williams.*
Hall, J. Earl	1867	*Hamilton.*
Hall, Edwin	1868	*Middlebury.*
Halsey, Calvin C.	1844	*Williams.*
Hanna, George L. C.	1866	*Madison.*
Hanna, William T. C.	1870	*Madison.*
Hamblen, Samuel	1862	*Waterville.*
Hamblen, Isaac S.	1858	*Waterville.*
Hamilton, Laurentine	1850	*Hamilton.*
Hamilton, Gavin L.	1857	*Rochester.*
Hamilton, Milton J.	1866	*Jefferson.*
Hamlin, Cyrus	1861	*Waterville.*
Hamlin, Edward O.	1850	*Hamilton.*
Hamlin, Charles H.	1858	*Hamilton.*
Hand, Elias	1845	*Union.*
Hannay, John S.	1839	*Union.*
Harlow, Edwin A.	1860	*Bowdoin.*
Harmon, Edward E.	1862	*Waterville.*
Harmon, S. S.	1840	*Union.*
Harmon, H. W.	1860	*Waterville.*

Herrick Hubert P.	1849	*Amherst.*
Herrick, Thomas P.	1856	*Amherst.*
Herrick, Henry	1858	*Williams.*
Herrick, Samuel E.	1859	*Amherst.*
Herron, Jr., David	1851	*Union.*
Hewitt, Charles E.	1857	*Rochester.*
Hickok, William C.	1845	*Union.*
Hickock, Elisha P.	1866	*Madison.*
Hickey, Yates	1849	*Hamilton.*
Hicks, Frederick	1861	*Williams.*
Higgins, Lucius	1860	*Amherst.*
Higgins, John S.	1855	*Rochester.*
Higgins, C. W.	1849	*Williams.*
Higley, Alfred E.	1868	*Middlebury.*
Higley, Edwin H.	1864	*Middlebury.*
Higley, Henry P.	1860	*Middlebury.*
Higley, George T.	1857	*Amherst.*
Hill, Lysander	1858	*Bowdoin.*
Hill, Samuel N.	1840	*Williams.*
Hills, John P.	1837	*Williams.*
Hills, William	1841	*Williams.*
Hills, Seth E.	1851	*Hamilton.*
Hills, Milton T.	1855	*Hamilton.*
Hindman, Thomas	1865	*Jefferson.*
Hitchcock, Milan H.	1854	*Amherst.*
Hobart, Anson L.	1836	*Williams.*
Hodges, George	1855	*Williams.*
Hodges, Willard	1845	*Williams.*
Hodgman, Thomas M.	1838	*Union.*
Holloway, Charles H.	1854	*Amherst.*
Hollister, John Q. A.	1862	*Hamilton.*
Hollister, Horace H.	1862	*Hamilton.*
Hollister, Martin F.	1867	*Hamilton.*
Holmes, Jesse M.	1855	*Union.*
Holmes, Daniel W.	1863	*Middlebury.*
Holmes, Richard S.	1862	*Middlebury.*
Hood, Robert	1861	*Union.*
Hopkins, Henry H.	1838	*Union.*
Horton, Marcus N.	1855	*Williams.*
Hosford, H. B.	1843	*Williams.*
Hosford, J. Manning	1847	*Williams.*
Hough, Lewis S.	1839	*Union.*
Hough, George W.	1855	*Union.*
Houghton, Jonathan S.	1857	*Waterville.*
Houston, James	1839	*Union.*
Howard, Daniel M.	1858	*Middlebury.*
Howard, James B.	1849	*Williams.*
Howard, Martin S.	1855	*Amherst.*
Howes, Roland S.	1838	*Williams.*
Howe, George M.	1850	*Union.*

Johnson, E. G.	1842	*Williams.*
Johnson, Edwin R.	1863	*Rochester.*
Johnson, Norman L.	1852	*Williams.*
Johnson, Hiram E.	1849	*Hamilton.*
Johnson, William J.	1850	*Union.*
Johnson, J. W.	1858	*Union.*
Johnston, James W.	1862	*Union.*
Jones, John M.	1867	*Western Reserve.*
Jones, Clinton	1860	*Amherst.*
Jones, Henry W.	1857	*Amherst.*
Jones, George O.	1869	*Washington.*
Jones, R. Elvin	1860	*Waterville.*
Jones, Thomas W.	1864	*Rutgers.*
Jordan, Edward M.	1840	*Williams.*
Joslin, George E.	1861	*Middlebury.*
Judd, Jonathan S.	1839	*Williams.*
Julian, Ernest	1869	*Western Reserve.*
Keene, Jr. Luther	1859	*Amherst.*
Keene, George A.	1860	*Amherst.*
Kenney, Joseph	1848	*Williams.*
Kehoo, John	1851	*Union.*
Keirsteed, Winkoop	1839	*Union.*
Keith, William A.	1841	*Williams.*
Kelley, William	1838	*Union.*
Kellogg, E. William	1836	*Williams.*
Kellogg, Henry	1843	*Williams.*
Kellogg, Allyn S.	1846	*Williams.*
Kellogg, Lauren	1845	*Union.*
Kellogg, Henry M.	1858	*Amherst.*
Kellogg, George W.	1859	*Hamilton.*
Kellog, William S.	1865	*Rochester.*
Kellom, John H.	1842	*Williams.*
Kendall, John F.	1855	*Hamilton.*
Kennedy, Joshua	1840	*Union.*
Kennedy, E. S. T.	1868	*New York.*
Kent, Evarts B.	1865	*Middlebury.*
Kenyon, William C.	1838	*Union.*
Kenyon, William H.	1865	*Rochester.*
Kerr, George	1839	*Williams.*
Kerr, William	1850	*Williams.*
Ketchum, Heber A.	1866	*Western Reserve.*
Keyes, Richard G.	1848	*Hamilton.*
Keyson, S. Cadney	1866	*New York.*
Kezar, Abner H.	1864	*Waterville.*
Kiehle, D. L.	1861	*Hamilton.*
Kies, Henry	1852	*Amherst.*
Kilburn, John A.	1852	*Williams.*
Kimball, Charles A.	1854	*Amherst.*
Kimball, John C.	1854	*Amherst.*
Kimball, James P.	1865	*Hamilton.*

Lassell, Nath'l	1839	*Williams.*
Lassell, Josiah	1844	*Williams.*
Lassell, S. M.	1844	*Williams.*
Laughlin, John W.	1861	*Jefferson.*
Laverty, J. C.	1851	*Union.*
Lawrence, B. F.	1858	*Waterville.*
Lawrence, George E.	1867	*Middlebury.*
Leach, Henry C.	1870	*Madison.*
Leavitt, George R.	1860	*Williams.*
Leavitt, Levi R.	1860	*Bowdoin.*
Leavitt, Jonathan G.	1863	*Waterville.*
Lee, J. Edwards	1841	*Williams.*
Lee, George	1868	*Western Reserve.*
Lefevere, Jonathan	1842	*Williams.*
Legate, Wm. M.	1839	*Williams.*
Legate, William M.	1838	*Union.*
Lent, Daniel E.	1858	*Rochester.*
Leonard, Delevan A.	1859	*Hamilton.*
Leiper, Hugh Y.	1863	*Jefferson.*
Leutsinger, Henry	1864	*Hamilton.*
Leonard, Albert S.	1870	*Washington.*
Lewis, T. Willard	1847	*Union.*
Lewis, David N.	1862	*Union.*
Leyenberger, Joseph A.	1861	*Jefferson.*
Libby, Eben H.	1852	*Waterville.*
Lilley, Foster	1838	*Williams.*
Lillibridge, William M.	1869	*Hamilton.*
Lilly, A. H.	1848	*Williams.*
Lincoln, I. N.	1847	*Williams.*
Lincoln, E. L.	1855	*Williams.*
Ludlam, Isaac F.	1866	*New York.*
Lindsley, Phales	1839	*Union.*
Link, David	1854	*Rochester.*
Linsley, Joel	1856	*Amherst.*
Litchfield, Daniel C.	1853	*Amherst.*
Little, Jr., James	1841	*Williams.*
Livingston, G. M.	1849	*Union.*
Lloyd, William A.	1858	*Williams.*
Lockwood, L. C.	1837	*Williams.*
Lockwood, William F.	1838	*Union.*
Lodewick, Edward	1870	*Rutgers.*
Loomis, Elihu	1847	*Williams.*
Loomis, Henry	1864	*Hamilton.*
Lord, Edward	1843	*Williams.*
Lord, Henry E.	1848	*Williams.*
Lord, J. Brown	1855	*Amherst.*
Loring, Edward P.	1861	*Waterville.*
Lounsbury, H. A.	1847	*Union.*
Lovell, T. A.	1846	*Williams.*
Lovett, John W.	1866	*Middlebury.*

McClellan, A. B.	1854	*Union.*
McClelland, George	1840	*Williams.*
McConnell, William T.	1870	*Washington.*
McClure, Benjamin	1845	*Williams.*
Macomber, Sylvanus B.	1863	*Waterville.*
McCracken, Joseph	1845	*Union.*
McFarland, John A.	1846	*Union.*
Macferron, R. C.	1866	*Jefferson.*
McIntyre, Andrew	1849	*Union.*
McIntyre, George Robinson	1858	*Bowdoin.*
McKean, John A.	1868	*Jefferson.*
McKercher, Finley	1845	*Union.*
McKnight, Jr., D. K.	1867	*Washington.*
McKown, S. Hunter	1865	*Jefferson.*
McKusick, J. F.	1862	*Waterville.*
McKusick, Hazen P.	1866	*Waterville.*
McLaury, John F.	1870	*Rutgers.*
McLaren, William S.	1840	*Union.*
McLean, Alexander	1853	*Hamilton.*
McLean, James	1856	*Hamilton.*
McLean, John	1862	*Hamilton.*
McLeod, Hugh	1851	*Amherst.*
McMahon, Robert Todd	1860	*Jefferson.*
McMartin, Peter A.	1838	*Union.*
McMartin, Archibald	1838	*Union.*
McMasters, Joseph M.	1869	*Rochester.*
McMath, R. E.	1857	*Williams.*
McMath, Norman C.	1864	*Hamilton.*
McMynn, John G.	1848	*Williams.*
McNab, Peter D.	1845	*Union.*
McPherson, R. C.	1866	*Jefferson.*
McQueen, Jr., George	1846	*Union.*
McVane, C. D.	1840	*Union.*
McVickar, James P.	1862	*Jefferson.*
McWilliam, A.	1847	*Union.*
McWhinney, Jr., James	1865	*Rochester.*
Mead, E. Belcher	1843	*Williams.*
Meeker, L. M.	1844	*Williams.*
Meigs, Charles H.	1850	*Hamilton.*
Melvin, James W.	1860	*Jefferson.*
Merchant, Abel	1846	*Union.*
Merriam, Edwin E.	1858	*Amherst.*
Merriam, George F.	1861	*Amherst.*
Merriam, Henry C.	1864	*Waterville.*
Merrick, Lucius L.	1860	*Amherst.*
Merrill, Samuel L.	1845	*Williams.*
Merrill, Sidney S.	1850	*Amherst.*
Merrill, Willard	1854	*Amherst.*
Merrill, William A.	1862	*Waterville.*
Merriam, William E.	1850	*Williams.*

Morgan, Edward N. S.	1844	*Williams.*
Morris, Henry C.	1849	*Williams.*
Morris, Charles D.	1867	*Rochester.*
Morse, Alfred A.	1864	*Hamilton.*
Morse, Adiel S.	1855	*Union.*
Morse, Charles F.	1853	*Amherst.*
Morse, George S.	1854	*Hamilton.*
Morse, Frank L.	1857	*Waterville.*
Morse, Samuel B.	1861	*Waterville.*
Mowbray, Jarvis	1838	*Union.*
Munn, Benjamin F.	1853	*Williams.*
Murphy, John T.	1870	*Madison.*
Murphy, Chester P.	1870	*Washington.*
Nellis, Peter S.	1840	*Union.*
Nelson, Henry A.	——	*Hamilton.*
Nelson, Edwin M.	1868	*Hamilton.*
Nelson, John S.	1849	*Williams.*
Nelson, John W.	1838	*Union.*
Nelson, Daniel T.	1861	*Amherst.*
Nettleton, Frank E.	1862	*Williams.*
Nevins, Benjamin C.	1867	*Rutgers.*
Newbanks, John	1849	*Williams.*
Newcomb, George W.	1849	*Hamilton.*
Newton, John M.	1849	*Williams.*
Nichols, D. C.	1845	*Union.*
Nichols, John	1839	*Williams.*
Nichols, A. D.	1845	*Williams.*
Nichols, Nathan R.	1866	*Middlebury.*
Niles, William A.	1851	*Williams.*
Nixon, William	1865	*Waterville.*
Noble, William H.	1837	*Williams.*
Noble, Calvin D.	1864	*Middlebury.*
Nodyne, J. Oakley	1838	*Union.*
Noerr, Moses	1855	*Amherst.*
Norris, James F.	1863	*Waterville.*
Norris, Lewis E.	1862	*Waterville.*
North, George J.	1861	*Hamilton.*
Northrop, G. W.	1855	*Williams.*
Northrup, Luther H.	1851	*Williams.*
Northrup, J. A.	1840	*Union.*
Norton, Charles H.	1847	*Williams.*
Norton, George	1865	*Hamilton.*
Norton, Winthrop	1860	*Bowdoin.*
Norton, Marcus P.	1854	*Union.*
Norton, Franklin B.	1856	*Amherst.*
Norton, Ransom	1860	*Waterville.*
Nott, Charles C.	1845	*Union.*
Nott, John W.	1845	*Union.*
Noyes, George M.	1852	*Williams.*
Noyes, Eli P.	1862	*Waterville.*

Nutting, Isaiah H.	1846	*Williams.*
Oakley, C. B.	1864	*Rochester.*
Odell, Joseph	1857	*Waterville.*
Ogden Henry E.	1862	*Union.*
Ogden, Isaac G.	1849	*Williams.*
Ogle, Jr., John	1866	*New York.*
Olds, Alfred J.	1850	*Williams.*
Oliver, John M.	1868	*Washington.*
Orton, James	1855	*Williams.*
Osborn, Henry	1842	*Williams.*
Osborn, Ira P.	1843	*Williams.*
Osborn, Richard	1845	*Union.*
Ostrander, J. J. P.	1849	*Union.*
Ostrander, Luther A.	1865	*Hamilton.*
Owen, D. D.	1866	*Madison.*
Packard, Levi S.	1855	*Amherst.*
Packwood, Ebenezer	1856	*Rochester.*
Page, Lansford S.	1862	*Hamilton.*
Page, Merritt B.	1866	*Middlebury.*
Page, Theophilus	1838	*Williams.*
Page, Increase B.	1846	*Willlams.*
Page, Joel S.	1846	*Williams.*
Page, William L.	1854	*Hamilton.*
Painter, Charles C. C.	1858	*Williams.*
Palmer, Charles H.	1868	*Rochester.*
Palmer, William R.	1849	*Amherst.*
Palmer, Albert D. F.	1861	*Bowdoin.*
Palmer, David H.	1857	*Rochester.*
Palmer, Francis B.	1858	*Rochester.*
Palmer, Gustavus S.	1861	*Bowdoin.*
Parmele, Lucius B.	1864	*Rochester.*
Parmalee, Howard R.	1869	*Western Reserve.*
Parker, Horace	1860	*Amherst.*
Parker, P. G.	1838	*Union.*
Parker, D. McArthur	1857	*Hamilton.*
Parker, Joel	1824	*Hamilton.*
Parry, B. P.	1838	*Union.*
Parshall, S. T.	1839	*Union.*
Parsons, Curtis B.	1858	*Rochester.*
Parsons, Lauton S.	1846	*Williams.*
Parsons, James M.	1852	*Williams.*
Parsons, Andrew	1857	*Williams.*
Parsons, Ralph L.	1853	*Amherst.*
Partridge, Sylvester B.	1861	*Middlebury.*
Patten, William	1838	*Union.*
Patterson, George C.	1856	*Hamilton.*
Patterson, Robert A.	1857	*Rochester.*
Patterson, Robert C.	1854	*Rochester.*
Payson, Charles H.	1852	*Amherst.*
Pattengill, W. W.	1869	*Madison.*

Paxton, John Steele	1860	*Jefferson.*
Peabody, Charles	1838	*Williams.*
Payne, Sereno E.	1864	*Rochester.*
Payne, Henry N.	1868	*Hamilton.*
Peabody, John Q.	1848	*Amherst.*
Payson, E. R.	1866	*Hamilton.*
Peabody, Henry H.	1866	*Madison.*
Pearson, Samuel W.	1862	*Bowdoin.*
Pease, Nicholas	1870	*Rutgers.*
Pease, David	1838	*Williams.*
Pease, J. J.	1862	*Hamilton.*
Pease, R. D.	1870	*Rutgers.*
Peck, Ransom R.	1845	*Union.*
Peek, Alonzo P.	1859	*Rutgers.*
Peet, Lyman W.	1861	*Middlebury.*
Pendleton, Cyrus H.	1856	*Amherst.*
Penney, Charles F.	1860	*Bowdoin.*
Pepper, Elbridge	1853	*Amherst.*
Perkins, Sidney K. B.	1851	*Amherst.*
Perkins, Jr., Asa	1856	*Waterville.*
Perry, Hermon	1849	*Union.*
Perry, Henry T.	1862	*Williams.*
Peterson, E. H.	1854	*Union.*
Petrie, Jeremiah	1845	*Union.*
Phelps, Zenas M.	1839	*Williams.*
Phelps, John W.	1857	*Middlebury.*
Philbrook, John A.	1862	*Waterville.*
Phillips, James L.	1860	*Bowdoin.*
Phillips, Lebeus R.	1836	*Williams.*
Phillips, J. L. T.	1847	*Williams.*
Phillips, Bradley	1845	*Union.*
Phillips, William C.	1849	*Union.*
Pickett, Edwin J.	1854	*Rochester.*
Pierce, David S.	1849	*Williams.*
Pierce, J. Kirk	1869	*Jefferson.*
Pierce, Charles M.	1857	*Williams.*
Pierce, Edward A.	1858	*Williams.*
Pierce, Herman H.	1851	*Union.*
Pierce, Henry R.	1853	*Amherst.*
Pierce, James E.	1861	*Middlebury.*
Pierce, Levi M.	1860	*Waterville.*
Pierce, Mathew L.	1865	*Middlebury.*
Pierson, Arthur T.	1857	*Hamilton.*
Piersons, Nathaniel E.	1841	*Williams.*
Pike, Fred W.	1859	*Amherst.*
Pitt, William H.	1858	*Union.*
Pixley, Martin S.	1844	*Williams.*
Pixley, S. C.	1852	*Williams.*
Platt, William K.	1838	*Union.*
Poler, J. S.	1843	*Williams.*

Pomeroy, Lou Dwight	1868	*Hamilton.*
Pool, Charles H.	1863	*Rutgers.*
Pond, W. Irving	1847	*Union.*
Pond, Nathan C.	1856	*Amherst.*
Pond, Theodore S.	1860	*Hamilton.*
Pouleson, Elmer	1869	*Jefferson.*
Pope, Eben	1862	*Amherst.*
Porter, Henry M.	1857	*Middlebury.*
Porter, William Dodge	1850	*Williams.*
Porter, J. Jermaine	1840	*Union.*
Porter, Charles L.	1852	*Amherst.*
Porter, William P.	1848	*Williams.*
Post, Thomas	1858	*Williams.*
Potter, Franklin	1839	*Williams.*
Potter, William S.	1852	*Williams.*
Potter, Aaron,	1840	*Union.*
Pound, Edwin H.	1856	*Williams.*
Powell, Fred W.	1838	*Union.*
Powell, Isaac P.	1860	*Hamilton.*
Powers, Llewellyn	1861	*Waterville.*
Powers, Isaac	1856	*Waterville.*
Powelson, A. Vannest,	1864	*Rutgers.*
Pratt, David J.	1839	*Williams.*
Pratt, Albert M.	1850	*Williams.*
Pratt, Henry L.	1852	*Williams.*
Pratt, Llewellyn	1852	*Williams.*
Pratt, Hiram A.	1848	*Amherst.*
Pratt, Edward H.	1853	*Amherst.*
Pratt, Daniel J.	1851	*Hamilton.*
Prentiss, Norman A.	1854	*Amherst.*
Prentiss, Charles E.	1864	*Middlebury.*
Prescott, Moses J.	1857	*Waterville.*
Preston, George M.	1852	*Waterville.*
Priest, E.	1839	*Union.*
Prindle, Lyman D.	1847	*Williams.*
Procter, William H.	1863	*Middlebury.*
Pugsley, Eugene W.	1841	*Williams.*
Pugsley, Edward S.	1846	*Williams.*
Putnam, William D.	1849	*Williams.*
Putnam, Kendrick S.	1864	*Hamilton.*
Putnam, Charles	1847	*Union.*
Putnam, Willard J.	1859	*Amherst.*
Putnam, Willard	1860	*Amherst.*
Rand, Francis	1849	*Williams.*
Rand, William H.	1865	*Middlebury.*
Rankin, William B.	1852	*Amherst.*
Ranney, T. P.	1852	*Williams.*
Ranslow, Eugene J.	1865	*Middlebury.*
Ransom, E. J.	1866	*Middlebury.*
Rappelye, B. F.	1845	*Union.*

Rawson, Edward D.	1851	*Amherst.*
Raymond, Henry K.	1838	*Union.*
Record, Isaiah,	1862	*Waterville.*
Record, Stilman H.	1860	*Waterville.*
Read, Philander	1859	*Amherst.*
Reed, Albert C.	1860	*Williams.*
Reed, Edwin	1858	*Bowdotn.*
Reed, Charles H.	1853	*Williams.*
Reed, John	1848	*Williams.*
Reid, John	1870	*New York.*
Relya, Benjamin F.	1845	*Williams.*
Remington, William	1855	*Rochester.*
Reynolds, George C.	1861	*Williams.*
Rhienhart, J. Kelly	1859	*Rutgers.*
Rhodes, James F.	1867	*New York.*
Rice, Charles E.	1867	*Hamilton.*
Rice, William B.	1845	*Williams.*
Rice, John M.	1855	*Rochester.*
Rich, A. J.	1862	*Waterville.*
Richards, Charles E.	1860	*Rochester.*
Richards, Zalmon	1836	*Williams.*
Richards, Charles	1838	*Union.*
Richards, Charles F.	1855	*Waterville.*
Richardson, Gilbert B.	1853	*Amherst.*
Richardson, Henry J.	1855	*Amherst.*
Richardson, Martin L.	1856	*Amherst.*
Richardson, Daniel W.	1857	*Amherst.*
Richmond, William	1854	*Hamilton.*
Rideout, Reuben A.	1861	*Bowdoin.*
Riggs, Charles H.	1862	*Rutgers.*
Righter, William A.	1839	*Union.*
Righter, George William	1850	*Union.*
Rightmyer, P. M.	1839	*Union.*
Riley, Andrew G.	1842	*Williams.*
Ripley, Erastus	1840	*Union.*
Ripple, E. E.	1867	*Jefferson.*
Robb, Alex. J.	1852	*Union.*
Robbins, Ellison	1849	*Hamilton.*
Robinson, J. McR.	1870	*Western Reserve.*
Robinson, Rodman H.	1840	*Union.*
Robinson, George W.	1870	*Western Reserve.*
Robertson, William S.	1840	*Union.*
Robertson, Henry M.	1840	*Union.*
Robinson, Samuel T.	1863	*Jefferson.*
Robinson, R. C.	1839	*Williams.*
Robinson, William A.	1862	*Middlebury.*
Robinson, David H.	1855	*Rochester.*
Rockwell, Jarvis	1855	*Williams.*
Rockwood, Ebenezer	1859	*Rochester.*
Rockwood, George A.	1858	*Middlebury.*

Scott, Walter W.	1870	*Rutgers.*
Scott, James Herron	1867	*Jefferson.*
Scott, Winfield	1855	*Rochester.*
Scovel, Dwight T.	1854	*Hamilton.*
Scriven, Gardner	1846	*Union.*
Scudder, H. M.	1842	*Williams.*
Searle, Stephen	1848	*Union.*
Searle, Charles H.	1869	*Hamilton.*
Searle, Homer W.	1870	*Hamilton.*
Sears, O. Maynard	1842	*Williams.*
Sebring, A. J.	1859	*Rutgers.*
Sebring, Elbert N.	1862	*Rutgers.*
Sedgwick, James	1841	*Williams.*
Seeley, Frank H.	1863	*Middlebury.*
Seeley, Nicholas J.	1846	*Union.*
Segur, Seth W.	1859	*Middlebury.*
Selmer, Henry M.	1838	*Union.*
Senard, E. Dwight	1870	*Western Reserve.*
Severance, Milton L.	1859	*Middlebury.*
Severance, Martin E.	1870	*Middlebury.*
Sewall, Lyman	1838	*Union.*
Seymour, John	1851	*Williams.*
Seymour, B. N.	1852	*Williams.*
Seymour, John A.	1849	*Amherst.*
Shafer, J. Douglass	1866	*Jefferson.*
Sharp, Robert E.	1864	*Jefferson.*
Shattuck, Amos F.	1859	*Amherst.*
Shaw, S. Francis	1855	*Williams.*
Shaw, Archibald M.	1856	*Hamilton.*
Shaw, Judson W.	1858	*Waterville.*
Shaw, Charles P.	1855	*Union.*
Shaw, Henry H.	1865	*Middlebury.*
Shaw, Robert P.	1865	*Jefferson.*
Sheffield, Charles S.	1856	*Rochester.*
Sheldon, Charles B.	1847	*Williams.*
Sheldon, Stewart	1848	*Hamilton.*
Sheldon, David H.	1854	*Rochester.*
Sheldon, George W.	1863	*Hamilton.*
Shephardson, Lucius F.	1858	*Waterville.*
Shephardson, Joseph H.	1859	*Waterville.*
Shepherd, Frank	1856	*Williams.*
Sherman, Elijah B.	1860	*Middlebury.*
Sherman, Linus E.	1861	*Middlebury.*
Sherrill, Samuel B.	1858	*Amherst.*
Shields, William H.	1865	*Rochester.*
Shoards, Joseph H.	1868	*Madison.*
Shoecraft, M. J.	1845	*Union.*
Sibley, Tarrant	1843	*Williams.*
Silcox, William L.	1844	*Williams.*
Sill, Amos H.	1845	*Union.*

Snowden, R. Bayard	1854	*Williams.*
Somer, George F.	1870	*Washington.*
Somers, William C.	1845	*Union.*
Soule, Jona.	1857	*Waterville.*
Soule, Martin B.	1862	*Waterville.*
Southwick, Andrew J.	1851	*Union.*
Southwick, Augustus B.	1863	*Hamilton.*
Sparks, Comfort	1837	*Williams.*
Spaulding, Boardman C.	1864	*Waterville.*
Spear, Ellis	1858	*Bowdoin.*
Spelling, Henry	1866	*New York.*
Spellman, William C.	1861	*Williams.*
Spelman, James H.	1844	*Williams.*
Spencer, Julius	1853	*Amherst.*
Spicer, Ambrose C.	1850	*Union.*
Sprague, J. H.	1850	*Williams.*
Sprague, Ezra T.	1855	*Amherst.*
Sprague, Havilah M.	1858	*Amherst.*
Spring, Leavitt	1862	*Williams.*
Squier, Wesley	1859	*Amherst.*
Squire, G. Lafayette	1845	*Williams.*
Stafford, Thomas W.	1847	*Williams.*
Stafford, Samuel S.	1840	*Union.*
Stark, Edward De Roy	1853	*Hamilton.*
Stenger, William H.	1867	*Rochester.*
Stearns, Marcellus L.	1863	*Waterville.*
Stearns, Sargent S.	1862	*Waterville.*
Stearns, Edward P.	1864	*Waterville.*
Stearns, George I.	1849	*Amherst.*
Stebbins, Charles E.	1856	*Hamilton.*
Steele, Charles G.	1860	*Middlebury.*
Steele, John B.	1860	*Middlebury.*
Stephens, George Lee	1863	*Waterville.*
Stephens, Ansel E.	1839	*Union.*
Stevens, Henry M.	1859	*Amherst.*
Stevenson, John M.	1838	*Union.*
Stewart, Robert L.	1866	*Jefferson.*
Stewart, Thomas S.	1863	*Jefferson.*
Stewart, Wm. Francis	1865	*Jefferson.*
Stickney, Robert	1838	*Union.*
Stickney, Gardner P.	1858	*Amherst.*
Stiles, Reuben	1868	*Rochester.*
Stoddard, John B.	1838	*Union.*
Stoddard, Elijah W.	1849	*Amherst.*
Stone, George	1845	*Williams.*
Stone, Horace	1851	*Union.*
Stootkoff, Cornelius W.	1838	*Union.*
Stork, Charles A.	1857	*Williams.*
Storrs, S. John	1860	*Amherst.*
Storrs, James H.	1838	*Union.*

Tiffany, J. Osmond	1859	*Amherst.*
Tilden, Alanson	1853	*Hamilton.*
Tilson, Ambrose T.	1845	*Williams.*
Tinker, Edward R.	1844	*Williams.*
Tinker, Joseph E.	1857	*Hamilton.*
Titus, Wicks S.	1846	*Union.*
Tomlinson, George E.	1855	*Union.*
Tompkins, E. C.	1843	*Williams.*
Torrey, Francis A.	1861	*Hamilton.*
Tower, James E.	1858	*Amherst.*
Townley, Hugh C.	1858	*Rochester.*
Townsend, Julius S.	1848	*Williams.*
Tracy, Samuel M.	1846	*Union.*
Tracy, Albion P.	1856	*Waterville.*
Traver, Alvah	1851	*Union.*
Tripp, Bartlett	1861	*Waterville.*
Truair, Geo. Galitzin	1864	*Hamilton.*
Truesdale, Wm. H.	1867	*Rochester.*
Truesdale, George	1854	*Rochester.*
Truve, Theodore	1870	*Madison.*
Tucker, J. Judson	1854	*Williams.*
Tully, David	1846	*Union.*
Tupper, Horace T. S.	1855	*Union.*
Tupper, Henry	1859	*Amherst.*
Turner, George M.	1837	*Williams.*
Tuthill, James H.	1846	*Williams.*
Tuthill, M. Townley	1850	*Hamilton.*
Tuttle, Henry A.	1844	*Williams.*
Twitchell, Justin E.	1858	*Amherst.*
Tyler, John I.	1838	*Union.*
Vail, James H.	1849	*Union.*
Vail, Henry H.	1860	*Middlebury.*
Valentine, Philo G.	1852	*Union.*
Valentine, Roswell D.	1852	*Union.*
Van Alstine, Eldert	1838	*Union.*
Van Alstin, J. S.	1867	*Rochester.*
Van Arsdale, N. Hixon	1862	*Rutgers.*
Van Buskirk, Peter V.	1866	*Rutgers.*
Vanderbilt, Cornelius J.	1846	*Union.*
Vandervolger, J. V.	1839	*Union.*
Van Deusen, Edwin H.	1849	*Williams.*
Vandeventon, John C.	1870	*New York.*
Van Doren, J. Howard	1859	*Rutgers.*
Van Ness, Jacob H.	1862	*Rutgers.*
Van Stanvoord, John	1838	*Union.*
Van Vanken, Adam	1853	*Union.*
Van Vanken, F. V.	1855	*Union.*
Van Vechten, A. V. W.	1847	*Williams.*
Van Vechten, T. F.	1850	*Williams.*
Vedder, Charles S.	1848	*Union.*

Welday, David M.	1868	*Washington.*
Welday, William H.	1868	*Washington.*
Wells, Samuel P.	1838	*Union.*
Wells, Henry	1838	*Union.*
Wells, Benjamin	1839	*Union.*
Wells, David A.	1847	*Williams.*
Wells, William	1854	*Williams.*
Wells, Horace H.	1857	*Williams.*
Welton, Henry S.	1852	*Hamilton.*
Wenzell, Abner H.	1853	*Amherst.*
West, Jr., Charles Henry	1864	*Hamilton.*
Westfall, John H.	1836	*Williams.*
Westfall, Samuel D.	1860	*Hamilton.*
Weston, Joshua W.	1853	*Waterville.*
Wetmore, William W.	1861	*Hamilton.*
Wetzel, Samuel William	1867	*Hamilton.*
Whedon, D. P.	1845	*Union.*
Wheeler, Hiram	1838	*Union.*
Wheeler, Edward R.	1860	*Amherst.*
Whidden, John N.	1853	*Rochester.*
Whipple, Alden B.	1852	*Williams.*
White, Samuel J.	1839	*Williams.*
White, William J.	1839	*Williams.*
White, Lewis	1845	*Williams.*
White, William P.	1845	*Williams.*
White, James	1851	*Williams.*
White, Jasper M.	1858	*Waterville.*
White, Nehemiah	1857	*Middlebury.*
White, Washburn W.	1857	*Middlebury.*
White, George	1861	*Williams.*
Whitehill, John	1858	*Amherst.*
Whitford, William C.	1850	*Union.*
Whitford, Oscar F.	1856	*Union.*
Whitney, Milton B.	1849	*Williams.*
Whitney, George O.	1869	*Madison.*
Whittlesey, Charles	1840	*Williams.*
Whittlesey, Eliphalet	1840	*Williams.*
Whittlesey, Elisha	1846	*Williams.*
Whittlesey, Charles B.	1858	*Amherst.*
Wieting, Archibald	1838	*Union.*
Wigging, George W. F.	1860	*Waterville.*
Wight, Joseph K.	1843	*Williams.*
Wight, Jr., Marcus	1861	*Bowdoin.*
Wightman, J. N.	1839	*Union.*
Wilbur, Charles D.	1856	*Williams.*
Wilcox, Lyman F.	1842	*Williams.*
Wilcox, Daniel W.	1852	*Waterville.*
Wilcox, Julius	1858	*Middlebury.*
Wilcox, S. Darwin	1866	*Hamilton.*
Wild, Edward P.	1860	*Middlebury.*

Yeakle, Joshua K.	1849	*Union.*
Yeoman, Samuel	1862	*Union.*
York, Albert L.	1852	*Union.*
Young, P. D.	1838	*Union.*
Young, Abraham T.	1839	*Union.*
Young, Madison	1839	*Union.*
Young, John D.	1862	*Union.*
Young, Moses W.	1864	*Waterville.*

www.ingramcontent.com/pod-product-compliance
Lightning Source LLC
LaVergne TN
LVHW021428110826
845150LV00007B/2137